KIDS*and the* SINGLE MOM

REAL-WORLD GUIDE TO EFFECTIVE PARENTING

by
JENNIFER BARNES MAGGIO

Published by TLSM Publishing
11613 Newcastle Avenue, Suite A | Baton Rouge, Louisiana 70816
225.341.8055 | www.thelifeofasinglemom.com

Book design copyright © 2017 by TLSM Publishing. All rights reserved.
Cover design by Kedra Deggins

Published in the United States of America

ISBN-13: 978-1542869300

Dedication

*To every single mother who thought she couldn't make it,
but somehow is...*

*To a church that repeatedly astounds and amazes me with its support,
generosity, and love for the single mom. Thank you, Healing Place
Church.*

To the husband and children I never thought I deserved.

PRAISE FOR
KIDS AND THE SINGLE MOM

"Jennifer Maggio is passionate about coming alongside single parents. With wisdom and grace, she offers encouragement, along with practical help, to those in the midst of this parenting adventure."

—**Elsa Kok Colopy,** author of
*The Single Mom's Guide
to Finding Joy in the Chaos*

"Jennifer Maggio has crafted a solid resource to guide single moms into effective parenting. She addresses the most important issues parents need to master in such a way that doing it alone seems far less daunting. This great tool is a must read for single moms with kids of all ages."

—**Nicole O'Dell,** founder of
Choose NOW Ministries and
author of the Hot Buttons series

"Single moms can be effective parents of successful children. From a mom who has been there, *Kids and the Single Mom* is gentle encouragement and practical tips. Chapters and reflection provide healthy steps for mothers to cherish the moments and develop their own unique talents. Sharing from her own failures and victories, author Jennifer Maggio reminds us that we are far from alone—we are beloved by God who promises to be our ever present help."

—**Peggy Sue Wells,** author of
*Rediscovering Your Happily Ever After:
Moving From Hopeless to Hopeful
for the Newly Divorced Mom*

"As a church planter and pastor in an urban setting, I am constantly meeting single moms who come to our church feeling empty, wondering if anyone cares and feeling worn out. And while my heart is to help, I've never been a single mom, so a disparity lies between my story and theirs. And it's because of this disparity that I am extremely grateful for *Kids and the Single Mom*. The honest life-experiences and transparent stories she shares will help me convey to single moms I encounter that there is someone who understands their struggles and who can provide wisdom and insight along their journey. This book is a must-have for every pastor's and ministry leader's library. It will help us all be more effective in ministry."

—**Crystal Tullos**, Pastor of
StoryHeights Church,
Boston, MA

"God has given Jennifer Maggio a specific anointing to resource the body of Christ with tools to minister to single moms. In *Kids and the Single Mom*, the solid Biblical teaching equips single mothers with spiritual and practical wisdom to aim their children toward God's absolute best for their lives. The study is relevant to the single parent household and applicable to impact the lives of both moms and their children."

—**Melanie Stone**,
founder of *GrowChurches.com*

"During the years I spent as a single mother I searched bookstore shelves for the type of encouraging, Bible-based guidance that *Kids and the Single Mom* provides. Jennifer Maggio's passion for connecting single moms to the heart of our Heavenly Father is changing the culture of today's churches and is impacting the lives of countless children worldwide!"

—**Christie Love**, Founder & Executive Director
of LeadHer, www.leadher.org

"Growing up without an engaged and involved father has a lifelong impact on a child. Jennifer Maggio does a great job of helping single moms understand and address that impact."

—**John Finch**, Creator of
The Father Effect Movie

"Jennifer Maggio's voice echoes truth and hope to single mothers. Her wisdom, passion, and experience mixed with biblical principles create a practical study for every woman raising children alone. For personal or whole group study, *Kids and the Single Mom* is the perfect choice."

—**Shelley Pulliam**, Co-Founder and
Executive Director of *Arise Ministries*,
creator of *Survive 'N' Thrive* national
single mothers' conferences

"Jennifer has done a superb job of writing a book that connects with single parents and the struggles they face. She encourages them through this Bible study by being authentic about her own experiences and bases her book on the truth of the word of God. I would highly recommend this book for any single mom or single parent ministry."

—**Robyn Besemann,** author/speaker,
singer/songwriter, and member of
single parent family ministry team at
Assn. of Marriage and Family Ministries,
www.robynbministries.com

"*Kids and the Single Mom* is so important to the Christian single mother raising children in this day and age. When we are looking for the answers, as we feel like we are fighting for our children in a society that seems like it's winning, this could not come at a better time. But we know the word of God has the answers. This book gives us those biblical principles that we can easily incorporate into our lives. This will bless you and your children."

—**Marjorie Bostwick**, Founder,
Single Mom Revolution

"There is a quiet problem going on in the church that has not been properly addressed until now—single motherhood. All too often single mothers are overlooked as they suffer silently not even knowing how to ask for help. Jennifer Maggio's passionate commitment to begin a conversation about this issue and provide the solution is heart-warming, inspiring and transformational. This one-of-a-kind single parenting guide is such a blessing to the Body of Christ and therefore the world. Jennifer illuminates the way to walk through the social, emotional and spiritual challenges single mothers face with grace and love."

—**Ericka D. Jackson**, Evangelist,
Author of *Beyond Fearless*

"Jennifer Maggio has inspired and brought words of truth to single moms as she gets real in sharing the ups and downs of parenting single. Her authenticity jumps off the pages and embraces all of us who parent single while inviting us to celebrate the present, embrace the gift of motherhood, and trust in the One who provides for us in all seasons. Thank you, Jennifer, for encouraging all of us to walk the path of single parenting with joy and faith! "

—**Jennifer Finnegan**, Founder of
Single MOMM, www.singlemomm.org

"Jennifer Maggio's new book, *Kids and the Single Mom*, offers practical and biblical insight for every single mom who feels overwhelmed with the seemingly impossible task of raising children alone. Fortunately, moms, there is help and there is hope. And here is one resource that will give you both.

—**Herb Reese**, founder of
New Commandment Men's Ministries

CONTENTS

FOREWORD

I Understand ... He Understands More

I REMEMBER ONE SPECIFIC moment in my newborn son's life. I changed him, swaddled him, and then held him close. "Well, son, it's me and you against the world." The words came as a whisper, but the message was heavy on my heart. My son's dad was out of the picture. Yes, I had my parents but Cory wasn't their responsibility, he was mine. I wanted to trust God ... I really did ... but how? How could I trust that God would really be there for me when I couldn't see Him? When I didn't feel His arms of support holding me up?

As I write this I'm now married with four kids. My husband adopted my oldest son, we had two more children together, and we also adopted a baby girl. But as I read Jennifer's story, her words took me back. I remember the fear, the frustration, and the little things my son did—simple childish things—that would put me on edge. Her story could be my story. And maybe your story is similar to ours.

The hardest part about being a single mom was feeling so alone. Every decision was mine. I didn't have money or resources. I had no magic mirror to give me a glimpse into the future. It was one of the hardest seasons of my life. Yet, in the way God works, it was also a season I needed to walk through. It was during one of the darkest days that I turned to Jesus. It was through the tears that I felt His comfort. And in every weakness I found out Jesus could be strong in me, through me.

It was on my journey I discovered this verse:

"But he said to me, 'My grace is sufficient for you, for my power is made perfect in weakness.' Therefore I will boast all the more gladly about my weaknesses, so that Christ's power may rest on me." (2 Corinthians 12:9 NIV)

If I hadn't been weak as a single mom, I never would have discovered how truly strong Jesus is.

Is single parenting hard? Yes. Are there days I wish I would have done things differently? Yes. Do I regret having a son when I was a teenager? No. I could never regret the gift my child is to my life. Were there days I wished I had more help, more support, more encouragement. Yes, yes, and yes. And thankfully Jennifer Maggio has written a book to help with all those things. Dive into these pages and you will find help. You will find support. You will find encouragement. Jennifer does it by sharing her heart and life. She's transparent, and I love that! She doesn't hide her bad decisions, actions or attitudes, and I love that, too! Instead she spills her guts and opens her heart, and then she points to God's Word. "I messed up," I can almost hear her whispering through the pages, "but see ... see how God changed everything."

Do you want to be an effective parent? You've come to the right book. Do you want to realize even greater what God can do for you during this season in life? You'll find the answers here. Maybe life didn't turn out like you planned, but I have good news. God's plans for your future are perfect. Allow Jennifer to help you discover those plans. I know you won't be disappointed.

Tricia Goyer, author of 32 books, including *Blue Like Play Dough: The Shape of Motherhood in the Grip of God*
Tricia Goyer

www.triciagoyer.com

INTRODUCTION

*"I was exhausted, financially broken, emotionally ruined,
and oftentimes felt I could not go on...."*

In my nearly two decades of parenting, I have made some grave mistakes. I have screamed and thrown temper tantrums probably more than my own children, at times.

I think back to my years of parenting alone. I was a scared, young teenager who had no idea how to take care of a baby. "Someone should still be taking care of me," I often thought. But that wasn't the case, and I was left with no choice but to learn to cook, clean, prepare diaper bags for the daycare, sing lullabies, balance a household budget, and so much more.

I was exhausted, financially broken, emotionally ruined, and oftentimes felt I could not go on. I took out my frustration on my children. When my sweet, innocent baby boy was only 4 years old, I was sick of sojourning as a single parent—sick of no one understanding how little money I had, how I could never get ahead, sick of not knowing the whereabouts of my so-called boyfriend and making excuses for him, and sick of having no help. I was going to lose it if one more person said, "I can sympathize. I feel like a single mom sometimes." My young son came to me and was quite whiny one particularly difficult afternoon. Before I knew it, I had slapped him across his little face and blood came gushing from his nose. I had busted my 4-year-old's nose. *What had I done?!* I was a terrible parent. I hated myself for all my inadequacies, for my failures as a mom, and for the fact that my children did not have the life they deserved. And now ... *this!* It brings tears to my eyes even now.

How can I admit that to you now? Because I am totally and completely free. I am free of the feelings of guilt. I am living in the freedom of it all. Sure, I messed up. I blew it. And there will be days when you do, too. But God's mercy and grace will be right there to catch you.

Somehow, through the myriad of bad decisions and mistakes, I sit here thinking of my almost adult children and how well they have turned out. I praise God for His hand of grace over our lives.

My son is a gifted athlete—charismatic, handsome, and funny. My daughters are equally as talented and beautiful, both displaying the joy that only comes from the Lord.

Many nights, I spent hours on my knees praying—praying for peace in my home, praying for God to help us, and praying over my children for them to be wise with their decisions. We are not to the end of our journey yet. But I want to take this opportunity to encourage you that the mistakes I made as a parent didn't "ruin" my children. And many of you need to hear that. Many of you have felt guilt rise up within you over a past mistake. Do not allow those feelings to hold you captive any longer. Your desire to seek after your Heavenly Father will keep your children safe.

I have been confident enough through the years to apologize to my children many times and they have turned out to be wonderful, God-fearing, obedient children.

I am no longer a financially destitute single mom. I am a happily married wife and mother of three. But I would not trade one second of those tough, almost unbearable years. Why? Because I may never have been able to witness first-hand one of God's mighty miracles—the transformation of my own life.

I received an especially sweet treat this morning. My 5-year-old and I were awake before the rest of the family and she climbed into my lap. She began to hug me and tell me that I was the "bestest mommy in the whole world."

Priceless.

May you be blessed, encouraged, and challenged with every turn of these pages.

CHAPTER 1

THE "I" IN PARENT

*"Take time for yourself. Constantly evaluate where you are
emotionally. Your emotional stability and spiritual
growth contribute directly to your overall parenting success."*

There is not a mother alive who does not agree that parenting takes hard work and plenty of energy. You can read every parenting book available, attend the most effective parenting seminars, and talk to the best parents you know ... and still have unanswered questions! Motherhood is not for the fainthearted. It is not for the weak. Add the fact that you are a single parent to the mix and it is twice as difficult and overwhelming.

Motherhood is a gift. It truly is a gift—a divine blessing. But no matter how big the blessing, the challenge is just as big. Prayer, diligence, and hard work surely abound in every successful mother. As the mother of two teenagers and a 5-year old, suffice it to say that life around the Maggio home can be quite interesting. One minute I am battling my teenage daughter over the latest fashion trend, the length of her shorts, or how to behave more lady-like. The next, I am singing "The Itsy Bitsy Spider" to my little one as she drifts off to sleep.

Despite the hectic schedule and occasional bumps in the road, I have learned some things on the journey that I believe are non-negotiables in the pursuit of successful parenting. The key is asking yourself some important questions.

- Am I enjoying my current season?
- Do I realize that God put a gift inside me, and am I pursuing it?
- Do I feel good enough—worthy of love?

Each of these questions pertains directly to you, the parent. Surprised? In my years of ministry, many moms have come to me with parenting woes and asked me for advice. I suspect that many expect me to rattle off a litany of rules, such as "bedtime at 8:00 p.m.; spank, don't spank; allowance, no allowance; etc." And sometimes we do explore those things. More often than not, however, when we begin to unpack the questions above, there is often a gaping hole within us in at least one of the areas. It never ceases to amaze me that once we moms commit to work on *ourselves* and *our* emotional well-being, our parenting skills improve dramatically.

Let's look at the first question:

Am I enjoying my current season?

You may be thinking: *Yeah right.* I never expected to be here. I never expected to be a single parent. My life was supposed to be different. I was supposed to have the white picket fence, the two rosy-cheeked, beautiful, happy children, and the adoring husband who worked hard, loved the Lord, and had eyes only for me. For whatever reason, that is not your current reality. Whether you lost your husband to a terrible tragedy, were never married, or found yourself the victim of a bitter divorce, I dare not paint you all with the same brush. I know that each journey has been different. The struggles may have looked different for each of you.

Some of you may be reading and thinking that the beautiful children that you once prayed that God would give you have now become your most difficult challenge. You have lost your joy. You have lost your vigor, spunk, and energy.

"For everything there is a season, a time for every
activity under the sun." (Ecclesiastes 3:1)

Oh, King Solomon's famous words in Scripture. To everything there is a season. Everything. *Wow.* He goes on to say in the next seven verses that there are seasons to plant, harvest, cry, laugh, speak, and be quiet. You must first realize what season you are in. Some of you have been in mourning for many years now. You have mourned the loss of what once was and the fact that it no longer exists in your present reality. You have cried yourself to sleep more often than not. You have hurt. You have ached. You have been restless, exhausted, and weary.

But, parents, now is your season to rejoice, laugh, dance, reap, and harvest! Do not look to what has been. Today, right now, recognize what is to come. Recognize that the joy of the Lord truly is your strength. The hurt of yesterday is left there, at yesterday, just waiting for you to let it go. Do not live in its tragedy, for it most certainly will remain as long as you let it. Rather look to the joy of your tomorrow—the future that starts **right now**.

I know it is hard to believe now, but that whiny 4-year old or that colicky infant will indeed one day be a graduating senior on his way to college. And trust me when I tell you that time flies. I still remember the day I held my bouncing 9-pound, brown-eyed, baby boy in my arms for the first time. I remember those early years when he never slept, cried way too much, and got into everything. I reminisce on his first day of school, his first basketball game, and the first time he drove the car down the driveway without me in it. We are now embarking on a new phase of life as he contemplates his college major, where he will live, and the life he will soon lead as an adult. The days have passed all too quickly. And they will for you, too.

When I was in the hospital, after having delivered him, I could not believe I was a mom. It was too much to think about. Someone was going to actually call me "Mom." *Me.* I do not remember ever having held a newborn in my arms prior to giving birth to him. I felt so ill-equipped. When the nurses finally brought him to me, I could not take my eyes off him. He was absolutely adorable ... and chubby, chubby, chubby. He only cracked his eyes open a couple of times while we were in the hospital. I barely knew what color they were. The first night I had him home I was telling a friend how I wish he would open his cute little eyes and look at me. I was extremely anxious to have that storybook moment that I had heard so much about when Mom and baby gaze lovingly into each other's eyes.

At about 11:00 p.m. that night, I got my wish. I peeked under the blanket to give him a quick peck on the cheek before putting him in his crib and there he was staring up at me. His big brown eyes were looking at me ... and it was not long thereafter that I regret-ted ever having asked to see them! He cried all night the first night we were home, and the second, and the third. And I know that people think I am joking when I say that that kid did not sleep the first three years of his life, but I am not. He didn't. He would cry and I would cry. Why didn't this baby sleep? No one told me that babies do not sleep.

Not long after my infant and I settled into a routine I found out that I was pregnant again. *Was I crazy?* Two screaming babies as a single mother?! I think I cried every day of that 10-month preg-nancy. (Yes, you read correctly. I was pregnant 44 weeks with that second baby. And yes, she was fat and adorable, too.) I gave birth to my precious baby girl and went to work two days later. I had no choice. My job offered no sick leave or vacation time. I worked full-time during the day and went to college full-time at night. All the while, I was caring for those two little ones alone, learning as I went.

And, for all the exhaustion and endless sleepless nights, what I would not give to rewind the hands of time and hold those precious children in my arms one last time! My point? For every dark moment that I experienced as a young mom with two children, there were a hundred bright moments—baby's first steps, first words, rocking them to sleep as I sang lullabies. Enjoy your season, for one day it will be gone.

"This is the day the Lord has made. We will rejoice and be glad in it." (Psalm 118:24)

Today is the day that the Lord has orchestrated for you, in your single parenthood, with your children, even in the midst of your struggle. He has not been surprised by your current circumstance. He has not scratched His head wondering what He will do next. He is completely in control of your life. He is able. He is sufficiently equipped to handle your trials and troubles. He has not left you. He promises that these troubles (although daunting at times) will not overtake you.

"When you go through deep waters, I will be with you. When you go through rivers of difficulty, you will not drown. When you walk through the fire of oppression, you will not be burned up; the flames will not consume you. For I am the Lord, your God, the Holy One of Israel, your Savior." (Isaiah 43:2-3)

He promises that there is not one thing that will completely over-take you in this life. Your child's disobedience, your struggles at work, or your ability (or inability) to make ends meet do not determine the magnitude of God's plans and purposes for your life. Enjoy your season with your children. Embrace where you are in your life right now. Understand that even if you parent alone for 18 years, it will only be 18 years of your 70-plus-year life. Choose to rejoice.

Take time for yourself. Constantly evaluate where you are emotionally. Your emotional stability and spiritual growth contribute directly to your overall parenting success. Recognize that this season of parenting alone is just that—a mere season. It will pass, whether it be when you get married or simply when your child becomes an adult, it is a window of time that you will surely look back on more quickly than you expect. Do not let those memories be about what you did wrong but rather about what you did right.

Parenting is full of ups and downs and learn-as-you-go moments, but what a joyful honor with rich rewards our Heavenly Father has bestowed upon us!

The next question we must ask ourselves as parents is:

Do I realize that God put a gift inside me and am I pursuing it?

Do you realize that there are plans that you have been put on this earth to fulfill and only you can do them? Do you realize that when your Father created you He did so with great intention with just the perfect plan for your physical features, your personality, and your abilities? What does any of this have to do with your parenting? Good question.

Do you remember when you were a little girl and dreamed of becoming the next world-champion figure skater or the next President or a teacher at the local high school? Do you remember how exciting it was to dream of your future husband and your future house? Do you remember the anticipation you felt? When did you lose that?

As parents, we do our very best to encourage our toddler and young children that they can be anything, do anything. They can become an NBA player, an astronaut, a doctor, or a scientist. They can discover the cure to cancer, the next dance move, or the remains of an ancient civilization. We speak life and truth to them. We encourage them. We push them and inspire them.

When did we lose that vision and dream for our own lives? When did we let it die?

For many of us, the insurmountable disappointments of life have replaced our once all-consuming dreams. The fire and passion that God placed inside of us to accomplish that thing that we knew we were placed here to do—own our own business, become a beautician, start a Bible study—has been quenched. It sits smoldering in the recesses of our minds. Dare we speak it? No. We dare not even think of that thing God put there. What if we are just setting ourselves up to fail? To be disappointed again?

Parents, listen closely. The very best thing you can do to help your child achieve his or her dream is to achieve your own. Show your child that against all odds you made it. You did not give up. You pursued. You persevered. You pressed in and pressed on. You become the next 45-year-old graduating college senior. You become the first in your community to launch a single parent ministry. You become the dark horse who rose to the top of Corporate America with drive and determination. As you begin to embrace your dreams, recognize that temporary setbacks are not permanent obstacles.

Maybe you cannot do the thing that God once called you to do in the same way you thought He called you to do it Maybe you cannot move to China with your 4-month old to become a missionary. So maybe your mission field never was China. Maybe it was always Small Town, USA, and you are now being mobilized and equipped to start that soup kitchen, that community outreach, that Bible study group. Dare to dream big. Dare to dream new dreams. Dare to ask the Creator for something bigger than you could ever think or imagine. And teach your children what it is to truly embrace their God-given dream.

And the last question we must ask ourselves as parents is:

Do I feel good enough—worthy of love?

This one is heavy. The emotional scars of a failed relationship can take their toll. And let's be honest. Not all of us lived the charmed life. I know that some of you arrived at single parenthood through no fault of your own. You have served the Lord as best you knew how, married as a virgin, and planned to be with your soul mate forever, until he came in and dropped the bomb on you that he no longer wanted to be married. I know that there are many of you out there who identify with that single parent. But there are some of us (like me) who made poor decision after poor decision when it came to relationships. We did very little right. We had sex outside the realm of the marriage bed. We had children outside of wedlock, and that shame caused emotional scars that, if we let it, can manipulate how we view ourselves.

I cry as I write, knowing that there are many broken women reading these pages. I know that some of you have allowed Satan to whisper in your ear that you are not good enough. You are not a good enough parent, a good enough sister, a good enough friend, a good enough daughter. You are not good enough. You are weak. You are *less than*. You are not worthy of love. If this is you, let me share with you God's truth.

*"I have loved you with an everlasting love. With unfailing
love, I have drawn you unto myself."
(Jeremiah 31:3)*

*"For I know the plans I have for you, says the Lord. They
are plans for good and not for disaster, to give you a future
and a hope." (Jeremiah 29:11)*

*"I have called you back from the ends of the earth, saying,
'You are my servant. For I have chosen you and will not
throw you away. Do not be afraid for I am with you. Do
not be discouraged for I am your God. I will strengthen
you and help you. I will hold up up with my victorious
right hand.'" (Isaiah 41:9-10)*

*"You have been my God from the moment I was born."
(Psalm 22:10b)*

*"Can anything ever separate us from Christ's love? Does it
mean he no longer loves us if we have trouble or calamity,
or are persecuted, or hungry, or destitute, or in danger, or
threatened with death? No, despite all these things, overwhelming victory is ours through Christ, who loved us."
(Romans 8:35,37)*

And there are dozens of other verses just like these. Your truth
is not how you *feel*. It is important that you understand that. There
are days when we do not feel very lovable. It is what we stand on.
There are days when we do not feel worthy. Yet God's word, His
truth, is that we are lovable. He has loved us with an everlasting
love from the beginning of time, and there is not one thing we
could ever do that would separate us from the fact that He loves
us deeply. Think about that for a moment. We are loved by the

One who has not only created the world but has overcome the death and destruction that lies here. That One loves us. He chose us. He hasn't forsaken us and He will never leave us. That's pretty powerful stuff.

Now understand that Satan comes to "steal, kill, and destroy." And for most of us, that is not in the physical sense. What he does is steals our joy. He kills our self-worth. He destroys our self-esteem. He whispers in our ear that the mistakes of our past will always define us. He tells us that the Lord could surely never love someone like us—as evil and sinful as we are. Do not listen to the lies! Consider the source! Cling to the *truth*—God's truth—that is your strength. Your wholeness comes in the word of God and in your relationship with Him. No other relationship defines you – not ones that have failed and not ones that are successful. The very essence of who you are is who Jesus says you are. End of story.

As you begin to embrace this reality as your truth, your perspective on your problems will change. You are "lighter on your feet." The weight of low self-esteem that has worn you down is now gone. Your victory comes in Christ Jesus and the sooner you understand that the more quickly you will succeed in your parenting.

REFLECTIONS on CHAPTER 1

THE "I" IN PARENT

1. Do you see parenthood as a gift? When is the last time you saw your children as a gift from the Lord?

_____

_____

_____

_____

_____

2. What are the three important questions that each parent must ask themselves?

_____

_____

_____

_____

_____

3. Why is it important to evaluate who we are personally in relation to parenting?

_____

_____

_____

_____

_____

4. Write Ecclesiastes 3:1 here. What does this mean to you? Are you enjoying your current season of life? Why or why not?

_____

_____

_____

_____

_____

5. What are some ways that you can begin to consciously enjoy your children no matter their ages?

_____

_____

_____

_____

_____

6. What is God's promise in Isaiah 43:2-3?

_____

_____

_____

_____

_____

_____

_____

7. Take time right now to write down where you are emotionally. What can you do to improve or continue your emotional stability?

   _____

   _____

   _____

   _____

   _____

8. What is the gift that the Lord put inside you? What are you doing to pursue it?

   _____

   _____

   _____

   _____

   _____

9. What is something you can do immediately to begin the pursuit of your dreams?

   _____

   _____

   _____

   _____

   _____

10. Do you feel worthy of God's love? Why or why not?

   _____

_____

_____

_____

_____

11. Read Jeremiah 31:3, Jeremiah 29:11, Isaiah 41:9-10, Psalm 22:10b, and Romans 8:35,37 again. Choose your favorite scripture and write it here. Commit to memorize it as truth for your life.

_____

_____

_____

_____

_____

_____

_____

_____

_____

_____

_____

_____

_____

_____

CHAPTER 2

LIVING AS AN EXAMPLE

"Do as I say, not as I do" just isn't good enough...

When I was growing up, my dad frequently said something that I am sure many of you heard when you were growing up as well: "Do as I say, not as I do." I am certain that in the 1930s, 40s, and 50s this must have been part of the standard training that every future parent underwent because I have heard it from most every parent I know of that generation. *Don't do as I do.* It is actually quite funny coming from my dad who, by the way, I loved very dearly. My dad suffered through a lifetime of hurt in a period of just a few years. He lost a son, a brother, and a wife (my mom)—all very unexpectedly.

The way he handled such tragic losses, however, left much to be desired. He used alcohol and women to mask the pain of his broken heart. You see, my dad married a total of six times, and that does not account for the girlfriends and mistresses in between and during the marriages.

Yet he was vehemently against many of the things he demonstrated in our home to his children. I remember the time he nearly had a heart attack when he found out my sister got drunk at a party as a teenager. In fact, I remember him banging around, screaming, and shouting profanities (with a beer in hand), when she confessed. The same was true when I finally shared that I was pregnant at 17 years old. I had hid the pregnancy for six months and finally mustered up enough courage to tell him, albeit by phone. I called him up and begin to speak, very cautiously: "Daddy, I am calling … ummmm … to tell you … well … to let you know that I am … uh … pregnant." I paused and braced for his unfavorable response. He didn't disappoint.

He screamed profanities and called me everything he could think of. He was furious, to say the least. He told me to "have a nice life," and from that day on I never lived in the family home again. Ironic, huh? The very thing he was so adamantly against—sex outside marriage—was the one thing he frequently displayed in our home from the earliest times I can remember.

If I had to choose one piece of advice, just one solid truth to stand on as a parent, it would be just the opposite of that old adage. EVERY single action you make, EVERY step you take, someone is watching you. Your children see. No matter how old they are, your precious little ones see your behavior and they will almost certainly duplicate it.

Have you ever seen a little 3-year old girl put her hands on her hips and shake her finger in the same way that her mother does or push a toy grocery cart? Have you seen a little boy pretend to mow the lawn just like his dad does with his "big" lawn mower? From an early age, children imitate what they see. The same is true for our teen and adult children. They most often behave as they have seen their parents behave in their own home.

Let's break this down into some typical, everyday examples.

None of us wants to see our children suffer with obesity, right? Yet many times we are guilty of indulging in one too many bowls of ice cream or too many fried foods, etc. In some cases, we even monitor what our children are eating, insisting they eat their fruit and vegetables, while we gorge on the latest gooey treat. I am not saying that having an occasional treat is wrong. In fact, if I'm being totally honest, I would tell you that I eat "occasional treats" pretty frequently. However, I exercise 5 times a week, rarely eat fried foods, and consume lots of fruits and vegetables. We know that scripture teaches that our physical body is our temple (1 Corinthians 6:19). And we know that taking good care of our bodies is important to the Lord. The example we display for our children is what they emulate. Statistics show that obese children most frequently come from homes where others in the home are obese. The same is true for other areas of our lives.

"Run from sexual sin! No other sin so clearly affects the body as this one does. For sexual immorality is a sin against your own body. Don't you realize that your body is the temple of the Holy Spirit, who lives in you and was given to you by God?" (1 Corinthians 6:18–19)

Because studies support that the majority of single-parent homes in our country are raising future single parents, we have to be especially careful in this area. Again and again we find biblical instruction to avoid sex outside God's design, which is in the confines of marriage. We see story after story of what havoc this sin wreaks in our own lives and in the lives of those in biblical times and the ultimate consequences of the sin. Yet many still choose this destructive path. There was a time in my life when I was so far off the path God had chosen for me that I couldn't even see the path anymore. Sexual sin was a real culprit in my life, so my words in this area are of concern not of judgment. I know the path of destruction that sexual sin paves. The choice to have children outside marriage led to many difficulties in my life that I know I would not have endured had I been obedient to God's word.

The same is true in your life. Obedience to God's word equals protection, not restriction. When the argument over abstinence arises (as it often does these days) in schools, the media, and elsewhere, abstinence is often presented as an outdated, old-fashioned tradition that no one could or would possibly want to adhere to. We are told that teens and adults will engage in sexual activity whether inside the marriage covenant or not, so why fight it? How awful that this is what many are teaching our children today!

Teen suicide among young women is most often linked to a male-female relationship that went awry. Many times, they were sexually active, the relationship failed, and the young woman was left devastated. How many times have you been left broken after a relationship with one to whom you gave yourself sexually failed? It is devastating. You are heartbroken.

The same is true for the practical side of abstinence, apart from our Christian faith. Sexually-transmitted diseases and unplanned pregnancies result from the behavior. Nothing our Heavenly Father commands is in some attempt to keep us bored and to suck the fun from our lives. It is to protect us, so that we can enjoy the beauty that is sex within our future marriage with a clean heart and clean spirit.

Parents, do not think you are fooling your children when you sneak Mr. Johnny into the house late at night convinced they are fast asleep and "in the dark" about your frolicking. Do not tell them as adolescents and teens not to engage in sexual activity when you cannot exercise self-control in that area. It is very simple. Ask yourself if your behavior is worthy of duplication. If not, then stop it. Sometimes that does not mean just sexual purity. Sometimes it means setting healthy boundaries in reference to a new relationship. Maybe for you that means no kissing before marriage. Maybe no touching is appropriate. Perhaps choosing not to be alone with the one you are dating is the best option for you. Pray about it and put in place guidelines that you would one day want your children to admire and choose to adhere to.

Honesty is another area that we must be diligent in teaching our children about by setting a truthful example. There is no such thing as a "white lie." Teaching our children early on that there are "fibs" and "white lies" only serves to blur the line between right and wrong. There are countless scriptures on honesty. Here are a few:

"The Lord detests lying lips, but he delights in those who tell the truth." (Proverbs 12:22)

"There are six things the Lord hates—no, seven he detests: haughty eyes, a lying tongue."
(Proverbs 6:16-17)

"Better to be poor and honest than to be dishonest and a fool." Proverbs 19:1)

"The king is pleased with words from righteous lips; he loves those who speak honestly."
(Proverbs 16:13)

"You must not testify falsely against your neighbor."
(Exodus 20:16)

The Lord requires that we be honest. That means that we are to be honest in **all** that we do. If we find money on the counter in the bathroom at work, we give it back. If we want cable or Internet in an additional room of our house, we pay for it. We don't steal it. If we find a grocery item in our cart that the cashier forgot to charge us for, we go back inside the store and make it right. We do not ask our children to advise a friend or neighbor that we are not home, when we are. We do not allow our children to stay home from school and then lie to the administration that little Pat was sick. We live our lives beyond reproach. We choose to live a life of high integrity. This is how we raise our children.

> *"And whatever you do or say, do it as a representative of the Lord Jesus, giving thanks through him to God the Father. Work willingly at whatever you do, as though you were working for the Lord rather than for people."*
> *(Colossians 3:17, 23)*

From the beginning of time, the Lord has chosen older generations to teach the younger how to live life in a way that pleases Him.

> *"I have singled him out so that he will direct his sons and their families to keep the way of the Lord by doing what is right and just." (Genesis 18:19)*

> *"Then, the older women will train up the younger women." (Titus 2:4a)*

The Lord's design for your family, whether headed by a single parent or not, is that you will raise up your child in the way that he would go. You are to teach. You are to train. You are to be an example before your children of right living.

Here are five questions that will help you identify areas in your own parenting style that may need improving:

- Am I speaking in a way that honors my children and my Lord?
- Would I want my children to one day choose this behavior?
- Do I adhere to "Don't do as I do....," or am I exemplifying the very heart of Christ?

- Do I behave the same way inside my home as I do outside my home?

- Have I repeatedly taught my children (through words and actions) that my relationship with the Lord is most important in my life?

Every time that parenting has been difficult in my own home and I have questioned what I am doing, if I am making good decisions, and how it will all turn out, I cling to Proverbs 31:28 that says that "her children stand and bless her." I am determined that as I parent my children, extend grace, and acknowledge my own mistakes with my children, they will one day stand and bless me for the mother I am. I pray the same thing for your household.

REFLECTIONS ON CHAPTER 2

LIVING AS AN EXAMPLE

Week 3:

1. Are there things currently in your life that you would not want your children to duplicate? How can you change them?

_____

_____

_____

_____

_____

2. Is there anything that your son or daughter does that others say are "just like you"? A facial expression? Certain word usage?

_____

_____

_____

_____

3. List 3 areas in which it is important that we raise our children up in the way they should go:

_____

_____

_____

_____

_____

4. Read 1 Corinthians 6:18-19. List 3 reasons why sexual sin is so harmful to our well-being.

_____

_____

_____

_____

_____

5. How can we teach our children about sexual purity?

_____

_____

_____

_____

6. Obedience to God's word equals protection *not* restriction. What does that mean to you?

_____

_____

_____

_____

Week 4:

1. Has there been a time in your life when it was particularly hard to be honest? Explain.

_____

_____

_____

_____

_____

2. Have you been guilty of teaching that little "white lies" are okay?

_____

_____

_____

_____

_____

3. Write Colossians 3:17, 23 here:

_____

_____

_____

_____

_____

4. How can you display "working as unto to the Lord" to your children?

_____

_____

_____

_____

_____

5. What are three of the five questions you can ask yourself to help identify your parenting style in reference to areas of improvement?

_____

_____

_____

_____

_____

_____

_____

_____

_____

_____

_____

_____

CHAPTER 3

FEEDING THE GREEN-EYED MONSTER

*"Single parents, whether widowed, divorced, or never married,
constantly struggle with the guilt that little Pat
does not have a two-parent home...."*

I was recently shopping at a local supermarket, calculating the cheapest price on the canned tomatoes, when I noticed it. It started out innocently enough. A 30-something mother was shopping with her two children, who looked to be between the ages of two and five years old.

"No, Matthew, don't put your hands on that," the mother told the little boy. He obliged, but only momentarily.

"Matthew, I said don't put your hands on stuff," she said, a little more authoritatively this time.

"No you didn't," the boy responded. "You said for me not to touch the peas. I'm not touching the peas."

"Well, do not touch anything!"

"I'm hungry.... I'm hungry.... I want some chips," the young boy whined.

Aisle after aisle, the whining and poor behavior continued, and endless threats abounded. "If you do that again, I'm gonna...."

Frankly, I was so sick of the whining and threats that I almost went over there to spank the kid myself! It just so happens that I checked out at the same time as the mom and her kids. And after much prompting by her little ones, Mom purchased two chocolate candy bars that the boys enjoyed as they left the store.

We've all seen it. Goodness, if the truth is told, we've probably all been that woman at one time or another—the one who overindulges our children, issues empty threats, and allows manipulation to prevail in our home. The fact is that many homes around the country, single and dual-parent families alike, are succumbing to the pressure of overindulging our children with gifts, toys, the latest gadgets, and more. For the two-parent home, maybe Mom and Dad are guilty because they work too many hours, or maybe they are simply trying to keep up with the Joneses.

For the single-parent family, it becomes ever more complicated. Single parents—whether widowed, divorced, or never married—constantly struggle with the guilt that little Pat does not have a two-parent home. We tend to romanticize what it would be like if his dad was around, how much better it would be, and how well-behaved he would be. The guilt consumes us. It leads us to make excuses. We whisper to our friends and neighbors things like, "Well, if his dad was around more...." or "He started behaving this way right around the time that his dad and I divorced."

Okay, there is no doubt that a divorce impacts a child. Numerous studies support that fact, so I am not trying to convince you that your divorce or the fact that Johnny has never had a father figure in his life is of no consequence. Of course it is. In fact, I will be addressing more about fatherlessness later in the book. But let's stop rationalizing that every tantrum is somehow tied to the fact that you are a single parent.

There are very few of us who cannot pick something devastating from our childhood and camp out there. Many have lost a parent at a young age, lived with an alcoholic, grown up poor, suffered through abuse, witnessed something we never should have, or experienced any number of other tragedies. But the fact remains that while those events may have shaped us, they do not have to *define* us. Your divorce, your failed relationship, or your deceased spouse do not have to define your child's future, either. We must parent effectively in the present, not blame our circumstances on our past.

It always amazes me to hear Moms who have been divorced many years still say, "Sherrie didn't start acting like this until the divorce." Really? When are you going to start holding Sherrie accountable for her behavior today? Again, let me be clear. I am not saying that the cause-and-effect that takes place due to the loss of a parent through divorce or a failed relationship is not significant. I know that it is. I have experienced it in my own life both as a child and as the parent of children who experienced it. And yes, those events do sometimes shape bitterness, anger, tantrums, and disobedience in our children's lives. But the fact remains that you are a single *parent*, however tragic your arrival here. This is where you are. And if you are going to reshape your child's future to ensure that he or she does not become yet another statistic, you must begin to teach your child to persevere, endure, and, frankly, to behave!

Parenting takes work—hard work. With discouraging statistics about the risks of single-parent homes, such as higher crime rates, lower education rates, higher abuse rates, higher likelihood of future single parenting, higher suicide rates, higher drug and alcohol addiction, etc. (*The Church and the Single Mom*, Carepoint, 2011), you have to work just that much harder. You must resolve in your mind now that your precious baby—the gift that God has granted you—will not become just another statistic. The world may say that your child will become one, but the transforming power of the Holy Spirit in your lives (and the resolve of a strong momma) can break any statistic!

Have you noticed how heavily guilt burdens us? Satan assaults us with that age-old lie that we will never be good enough because we failed in this area or that. We single moms are especially susceptible to this lie. We know that our child would be better-served in a two-parent home. And if you are anything like me, you know that you played a role in disrupting that two-parent dream. It is hard not to allow the guilt to gnaw at us from the inside out. Or maybe it is a different issue. Maybe you have to work two jobs for financial reasons and you have become guilty that you are not spending enough time with your children. Or maybe you feel guilty that you are not able to provide your children with those hot new name-brand tennis shoes on your limited budget. Whatever the case, guilt can be a real problem. Thankfully, the Lord has offered us real solutions.

"If we confess our sins, he is faithful and just to forgive us
our sins and to cleanse from all wickedness."
(1 John 1:9)

"He has removed our sins as far from us as the east is from
the west. The Lord is like a father to his children, tender
and compassionate to those who fear him."
(Psalm 103:12-13)

The Lord is faithful to forgive us when we have failed Him, so if you are burdened with guilt from a past mistake, allow His cleansing blood to wash over you right now. Accept the forgiveness that He offers to a repentant heart. He casts that sin from one end of the earth to the other never to bring it up again. Accept the forgiveness. So often we are forgiven by our Savior, yet we cannot forgive ourselves. Not one of us is without sin, fault, and mistakes, but our relationship with the King is what makes us different. He promises us freedom, so cast your cares upon Him.

If your guilt stems from long work or school hours, learn to embrace your season. (Remember this principle from Chapter 1?) Understand that your long hours at work or those extra classes you are taking at school are only for a season. I know that your heart is to be with your kids more. I know that you miss them when you are unable to tuck them into bed. (I have picked up my children many times after they were both asleep!) It is hard. But it is *only for a season.*

Sometimes the most important thing we can teach our children is the value of hard work and meeting financial obligations with integrity. That may mean extra hours at work this week, this month, or even this year. Remember to continue to be in prayer so that the Holy Spirit can work in your life and prompt you when the season is over. This is the key to living a life of balance in parenting (and in all other areas, too, for that matter).

Understand that parenting through guilt is not, and never will be, successful or effective. Throwing the latest video game at your child will not undo the fact that you are working long hours as a single parent. But what it will do, if you aren't parenting with intention, is exhibit to your child that he is somehow entitled to that video game because he is a "victim of divorce." This is a dangerous area, parents. The same is true when you throw that big birthday bash, knowing full well that you cannot afford the clown, the jump house, and the expensive bakery cake. These amenities will not compensate for the fact that his father isn't showing up to the party ... so stop trying. Try being honest with him instead. Learn to parent proactively. If your budget affords a party with a bakeat-home cake and a few close family members, then that is simply what you do.

The pressure that we all experience from television, movies, actors, and other relationships that somehow suggests that we are all to give our children everything they want, overcompensate when they are hurt, and abandon discipline has led to a deterioration of morals and values in our country like we have never seen. Our children are raised as victims of every kind—divorce, poverty, single-parent homes, sickness—whatever that thing is. We have begun to raise them as victims, subconsciously (or sometimes consciously), that they are somehow "owed" that toy, that candy bar, that name-brand clothing. We have created a generational sense of entitlement. The sooner you embrace wise parenting by releasing your past guilt and parenting with intention, the better.

The Bible is chock-full of tips on the parent-child relationship. I wanted to share a few with you here in hopes that you will begin to grasp the magnitude of your parenting privilege. I suggest that you read these and choose some to regularly share with your children, beginning at a young age. (Single mothers, be aware that in scripture many parenting instructions were given to fathers. You can easily replace the word "father" with "mother," as you are currently the head of your household, until such a time as God sees fit to bring you a spouse.)

> *"My child listen when your father corrects you. Don't neglect your mother's instructions. What you learn from them will crown you with grace and be a chain of honor around your neck." (Proverbs 1:8-9)*

> *"My children, listen when your father corrects you. Pay attention and learn good judgment." (Proverbs 4:1)*

"A wise child brings joy to a father; a foolish child brings grief to a mother." (Proverbs 10:1)

"Children, obey your parents, for you belong to the Lord, and this is right." (Ephesians 6:1)

"Only a fool despises a parent's discipline; whoever learns from correction is wise." (Proverbs 15:5)

"Don't fail to discipline your children. They won't die if you spank them. Physical discipline may well save them from death." (Proverbs 23:13-14)

"So give your father and mother joy! May she who gave you birth be happy!" (Proverbs 23:25)

"Direct your children onto the right path, and when they are older, they will not leave it." (Proverbs 22:6)

"To discipline a child produces wisdom, but a mother is disgraced by an undisciplined child." (Proverbs 29:15)

"Discipline your children and they will give you peace of mind and will make your heart glad." (Proverbs 29:17)

"A servant pampered from childhood will become a rebel." (Proverbs 29:21)

And there are many others. I love Proverbs and how it gets right to the point. Discipline your children. Parent with courage. Don't make apologies for your rules and boundaries. The Lord created us with boundaries and structure, so why should you make apologies for mimicking his design?

REFLECTIONS ON CHAPTER 3

FEEDING THE GREEN-EYED MONSTER

1. Have you ever had one of your children throw a temper tantrum in the grocery store or other public place? What did you do?

   _____

   _____

   _____

   _____

   _____

2. Have you been guilty of making excuses for your child(ren) in relation to your singleness? How so?

   _____

   _____

   _____

   _____

   _____

3. What are two areas in which a parent can sometimes struggle with guilt?

   _____

   _____

   _____

4. What does God's word say about our sins in 1 John 1:9?

_____

_____

_____

_____

5. Write here any area in which you have struggled to forgive yourself as a parent or a child of God. Then write a prayer to the Lord asking Him to forgive you and help you begin to accept that forgiveness.

_____

_____

_____

_____

6. Recall a time when you overindulged your child. Write it here.

_____

_____

_____

_____

7. Why is it important to acknowledge the overindulgence?

_____

_____

_____

_____

_____

8. How could you have handled the situation better? What will you do in the future?

_____

_____

_____

_____

9. Have you ever felt outside pressure to purchase your child something you could not afford? Why or why not?

_____

_____

_____

_____

10. Of the many parenting verses listed in Chapter 3, choose your favorite and write it here:

_____

_____

_____

CHAPTER 4

THE FATHER FACTOR

"I never fully understood the effects of the father factor on me personally or the importance of a father until I walked into ministry and began to counsel hundreds with similar stories."

My earliest memory is of an event that happened when I was approximately three years old. I heard a strange noise coming from the kitchen in the middle of the night. I grabbed my favorite blanket and proceeded down the hall. Upon entering the kitchen, I was surprised to find a great deal of scurrying to and fro among family and friends. To my horror, I looked across the room and saw my father's head covered in blood, as my stepmother began to wash him in the sink. Startled by my presence, a family friend assured me that everything was fine and quickly ushered me back to bed. I lay awake that night wondering what had happened and if my daddy would die.

I later learned that my dad had been driving drunk and wrecked his truck. I would like to say that this early memory was my only memory of my dad having had too much to drink or that drinking was his only indiscretion. I cannot. My dad made many poor choices over the years. But that did not make me love him any less. He was my dad, flaws and all.

In a desperate attempt to earn my father's love, I became a classic overachiever in high school. No matter how tumultuous my home life, I shined as the brightest star in my small high school. My dad beamed when I brought him a report card with all A's. He cheered and clapped when I scored a basket in my basketball games (albeit rarely). I wanted to *earn* the love of the first man I had ever loved—my daddy. And although I am certain he loved me, the fact that he did not exemplify a strong role model in my life took its toll on me. I began searching for love in all the wrong places and jumped from one dead-end relationship to another, always leaving empty. Ultimately, I wound up pregnant in high school. I hid the pregnancy for months because I could not bare to disappoint my dad. No matter how many times he failed me, I could not bear the thought of failing *him*.

I could site many stories of friends, family and church members, and those I have served in the ministry who have similar journeys. They had fathers who, by all accounts, failed them. They made poor choices. They beat them. They were not around very often. But none, not one, I have ever talked with has hated her father.

By God's design, the father was always supposed to be the head of the household. God looked at His first creation in Adam, as man, and said, "It is good." Scripture provides endless instruction to men as the head of the household on how to be a good husband and a good father. Yet, today, we find ourselves in the midst of an all-out war on family. Fathers have left the homes they were God-ordained to serve. Fathers have abandoned the children God gave them as gifts. Fatherlessness has become the breakdown of the family as we know it. We are seeing it more frequently than ever. And, more importantly, we are seeing its after-effects.

According to Mark Hall *(Fathers Manifesto)*, children from fatherless homes are:

- 5 times more likely to commit suicide
- 32 times more likely to run away
- 20 times more likely to have behavioral dysfunction
- 14 times more likely to rape
- 10 times more likely to use drugs or alcohol
- 20 times more likely to end up in prison

Wow. And that is just the tip of the iceberg. Pick up any newspaper and read about the latest crime spree in your community. A recurring theme is that the young men who are linked to the crime were parented in a single-parent home. Many never even knew their fathers. The anger and abandonment issues that result from fatherlessness are apparent. Those fully-functioning citizens who were parented by a single mom are now heralded as exceptional success stories rather than the norm.

I never fully understood the effects of the father factor on me personally or the importance of a father until I walked into ministry and began to counsel hundreds with similar stories. I was caught in that trap of thinking that I was an exception. I remember thinking that my own tragedies were rare. I mean, how could others have walked through these things? They were unspeakable. Yet, more and more, I realize that for every statistic cited and every number quoted, there is a face behind the number. There is a living, breathing person who has walked out the effects of a deadbeat dad in her life, a mom who is living with children who are now fatherless.

Don't get me wrong. Mothers have their place. We are the gatherers and nurturers. We are the ones who listen, pat heads, and kiss boo-boo's. We give the best hugs and the warmest smiles. We clean and organize better than the others. We plan and prepare. We nestle our children warmly in their beds. But too often mothers have had to step into a role for which they were never actually meant to fulfill. In addition to all their other duties, they have become the hunters, providers, and protectors. They have had to play both good cop and bad cop. They have had to discipline without support and decision-make without additional counsel. And many have done quite well. But the burden is heavy.

Is it any wonder that so many of us struggle to fathom the depths of our Heavenly Father's love?

He loves us with an unconditional, everlasting love. He will never forsake us. He is always with us and promises never to abandon us. He called us back from the ends of the earth and chose us as His beloved. We are His pride and joy. He smiles as He watches us. He is not mad at us or disappointed. He encourages us, upholds us with His mighty victorious hand, and protects us. He provides all our needs. He teaches us with warmth and compassion. He uses us even when we are certain that we are unusable. He forgives us even when we do not deserve it.

It is hard for me to even wrap my mind fully around that kind of love. It seems that no one has ever loved me like that. Yet my Heavenly Father—oh my Father! He loves me! He loves me more than I can comprehend, think, or imagine. He loves. No one can measure depths of His love for us. And although I cannot fully comprehend it, I embrace it anyway.

Maybe you are feeling a bit defeated as you read knowing that your son or daughter is without a father in his or her life. There are some steps you can take. First, and most important, accept the gracious love of your Heavenly Father as we talked about above. Honestly, I do not know how else we are to overcome the disappointments of this world, if we do not first have a heart that is open to the Lord Jesus.

Single parents, single moms, the only way that we can fully overcome the crisis that is fatherlessness in our country is through the blood of Jesus that washes over each of us. His word says that He is a father to the fatherless. If your reality is the lack of a father in your child's life, you cannot change that. You cannot make your ex-husband pick up his kids on weekends. You cannot make that absentee father desire to be part of his children's lives. You cannot make him be consistent and faithful. But you *can* teach your children about the everlasting love of their Heavenly Father. You *can* empower them with the word of God that assures them that they are good enough. They are complete. They lack nothing. You *can* parent them as best you know how and pray daily for God's divine wisdom to intervene where you fail.

But don't stop there. You can take it a step further. Teach your sons how to be fine young men. Teach them chivalry and do not buy into the myth that it is dead. Teach them integrity and honesty. Teach them that women are daughters of the King and should be treated as such. Begin early on having conversations about what it is to be a man of God, walking upright with the Heavenly Father. Teach them skills of provision. Show them courage. Teach them that filthy music that belittles women is unacceptable and teach them to deplore it. Do not compromise with television programs and movies that praise men who does not care for their children. Be strong in your parenting and teach your sons to do the same when they have their own children.

Teach your daughters similar things. Teach them that as daughters of the King they are to behave like royalty. Teach them that, as such, they are to use wisdom in their future relationships. Teach them to see a snake in the grass. Accustom them to expect their dates to open doors for them. Instill such high self-esteem in them that they immediately run from any young man who degrades them, speaks poorly of them, or does not hold them in highest regard. Teach them to run from any man with children who is not actively supporting them financially, physically, **and** emotionally and not make excuses for him.

Another way to counteract the father void that is left in your child's heart is to get them involved at the local church. That is a common theme with me, isn't it? Well, there is a reason.

> *"The human body has many parts, but the many parts make up one whole body. So it is with the body of Christ. But our bodies have many parts, and God has put each part just where He wants it. How strange a body would be if it only had one part!" (1 Corinthians 12:12, 18)*

We are all the body of Christ. We all have a role to play. There are children's pastors and youth pastors in your local church who have been called to help fill the void in your child's life. There are men and families in the body of Christ who can help provide mentorship, friendship, and instruction for your children. Hebrews 10:25 encourages us not to forsake the gathering of the body. There is safety there.

The Life of a Single Mom Ministries (of which I am founder) recommends several great organizations to help you on your journey.

Divorce Care for Kids (DC4K), founded by Linda Ranson Jacobs, is a national program designed to help children overcome divorce and to equip parents and ministry workers to achieve life-giving results with their children. DC4K is a special group that helps children heal from the pain caused by a separation or divorce. DC4K provides children with a *safe* and *neutral* place to recognize and learn to share their feelings. For 13 weeks children participate in a fun, caring group at a local church in your area. The weekly topics help the children learn that God's love strengthens them and helps them turn their sadness to hope and their anger to joy. Each session is filled with fun activities, including games, crafts, role-playing, discussion times, and journaling to help children process the divorce and move forward in their lives. DC4K is a powerful ministry for kids 5–12 years of age and can be found in local churches in nearly every community in the United States.

Additionally, **The Mentoring Project** (TMP) in Portland, Oregon, is on a mission to ensure that fatherless youth (not only in the Portland area but across the United States) are mentored by Godly men. The Mentoring Project is an advocacy and training organization that serves as liaison between faith communities and matching agencies to provide mentors for fatherless youth. Through dynamic church training, national mentor recruitment, and the creation of sustainable mentoring communities, TMP seeks to rewrite the story of the fatherless generation.

In keeping with its mission, TMP establishes relationships with local and national faith communities, partner organizations, and matching agencies to facilitate the creation of sustainable mentoring communities. It does not function as a matching agency. The Mentoring Project's model assists faith communities in establishing sustainable mentoring communities that will provide mentors for the children waiting to be mentored who can be found through well-established matching agencies such as Big Brothers Big Sisters

These ministries, along with dozens more, will assist you in getting your children the proper guidance they need and help you with raising your children the way God intended.

REFLECTIONS ON CHAPTER 4

THE FATHER FACTOR

1. What is your earliest memory of your own father? How has
   this affected you?

   _____

   _____

   _____

   _____

   _____

2. Does your child have an active father or father figure in his life?
   How does that make you feel?

   _____

   _____

   _____

   _____

3. Why do you think it is important to have a father in a child's
   life?

   _____

   _____

   _____

   _____

4. What is the one statistic that stood out most to you from Chapter 4?

_____

_____

_____

_____

5. What are some of the words that describe fathers as God design them to be when they are serving in their traditional roles? Mothers?

_____

_____

_____

_____

_____

6. Why is it important to understand and embrace our Heavenly Father's love?

_____

_____

_____

_____

7. How does our Heavenly Father's love differ from that of an earthly father (even a good one)?

_____

_____

_____

_____

_____

8. List two things you can do to help your children overcome a father void in their lives:

_____

_____

_____

_____

9. What are some practical strategies you can begin to implement immediately to achieve this?

_____

_____

_____

_____

10. List two organizations, in addition to your local church, that can help you on your single parenting journey.

_____

_____

_____

_____

CHAPTER 5

HEALTHY BOUNDARIES

*"Boundaries, simply put, are rules. They are parameters that
are ideal for your child, your home, and your situation."*

My first experience, or at least the first that I remember, of holding a new baby was that of my first-born when I was 18 years old. I had no clue what I was doing. I had never changed a newborn's diaper or fed one a bottle. I didn't know about diaper bags or warming bottles or colic, baby cereal, baths, and eczema. And the list goes on and on. But suffice it to say there was no shortage of advice-givers in reference to what I *should* be doing. So much so, that I did not even know where to begin. I was deathly afraid of making a mistake. I spent the first several months of my son's life lying awake staring at him to ensure that he did not stop breathing during the night.

As a single parenting expert (oh, I do not think I will *ever* get used to that term! I prefer being referred to as a girl who just loves single mommas, but anyway), I am frequently asked parenting questions. In my first book, I plainly say, "I am no expert." And I am convinced that few people truly are experts in the field of parenting. Yes, experience makes us wiser, but every child is different.

I continue to believe that among the best experts in the field of parenting are our very own aunts and grandmothers who have raised children, learned from their mistakes, and reveled in their successes. For the next few pages, I will share with you those parenting lessons that have made me wiser and the topics I am asked about most frequently.

My first two children were born 17 months apart. It seemed like they were born back-to-back. I was a single mom with both. I was only 20 years old when I gave birth to my second child. And I don't mind telling you that I still did not have much of a clue as to what I was doing. I was surviving. My first two children did not sleep through the night until they were well past three years of age. Yes, you heard me right. Three years old! Consequently, I missed about four years of cumulative sleep (which is still my excuse today if I am in a bad mood, so watch out).

By the time I got pregnant with my third child, I was almost 10 years older and married. I debated for years about having another baby. The lack of sleep alone was enough to make one never want another child. Alas, I made the leap and my husband and I were expecting our bundle of joy.

I gave birth and brought our precious angel home and, true to character for all my children, she never slept. Nights became a nightmare as I struggled to get out of bed with the little one. And, yes, I did have help this time around and my husband did, in fact, help. But all of you already know that when a mom hears her crying baby in another room, it is very hard to ignore (even as your husband is fumbling around in the dark, clumsily trying to soothe her). When my newborn was about three months old, I was ready to pull my hair out. I was simply exhausted. I was sleep-deprived, which made life seem pretty bad—not at all happy and joyful as the diaper commercials promised. And on top of everything else, I was sick of looking at my jiggly body, the bags under my eyes, and ... well, the endless list of other self-deprecating comments I could think of, so ... I decided to start running again at 5:00 a.m. with my neighbor. (It was a great idea for a postpartum depressed, sleep-deprived, new mom.) I was determined to get back into shape. Did I mention that my neighbor was a personal trainer? Yeah, her thin, fit body just made me all the more cranky. I must have been pure joy as a running partner in those days, as I cried many mornings from the lack of sleep (and wet myself many others from the lack of bladder control). But she hung in there with me, trained me for a marathon later that year, and taught me a valuable lesson that I will never forget.

After a particularly difficult, sleepless night with my then 4-month-old, I headed out for my morning jog. My friend and I talked about how exhausted I was all the time.

"Your baby isn't sleeping through the night, yet?!" she asked in amazement.

What was she talking about? Babies slept through the night? I thought they were at least toddlers before they slept all night.

"No," I muttered, "she isn't."

"Girl, I am about to give you some freedom.... and some sleep! Let me tell ya what ya need to do." And so it began. She unveiled the secret that apparently many mothers around the globe knew and practiced but that I was not privy to: *Your baby can cry and you do not have to instantly pick her up!*

Setting the Earliest Boundaries
New mothers, I am talking to you, here. Listen closely: *Your baby can cry and you do not have to pick her up!* Within two days of discovering this life-saving advice, my sweet infant was sleeping through the night! *Two days!* I could not believe it. It was heaven on earth. I lost 10 pounds, went back to work, and had a fresh outlook on life once she finally started sleeping. There are mothers

everywhere leaping from their seat as they read this, praying I will reveal "the secret." So here it is.

Once your baby has gone through the appropriate feeding adjustments (varies by baby, but usually 8-12 weeks), she will begin to self-regulate her feeding schedule. She begins to regulate her sleeping schedule, too. Unfortunately, for most babies, that means that they continue to wake themselves at night out of habit. Because Mom runs in to grab them immediately, it continues for months (or in my case, years). I suggest beginning this new method when your baby reaches approximately three months old. Be certain that you are feeding your baby the appropriate portion size during her nightly bottle, that her diaper is clean, and you have given her a bath. Once the baby is completely comfortable, fed, and clean, it is time for bed. The end. That's it. Now you know the secret. Your baby has the capacity *and the desire* to sleep restfully all night.

You must train her to do this. When she wakes the first night, you will have to make a conscious decision to let her cry. Do not enter the room. Do not talk. Just listen. Unless you hear some blood-curdling scream that indicates something is seriously wrong, do not answer the cry. Just let her cry herself back to sleep. I know. I know. It seems so cruel, especially if you are a new, first-time mom. But the reality is, the cruelest thing that many mothers are doing to their babies is not allowing them a full night's sleep. Train them early to sleep through the night and both you and baby will be thankful you did.

This brings up another point. Notice I said, "Do not enter the room." This assumes that your baby is not in the same room with you. I know there will be exceptions to this, because many single moms may still be living with parents or in small apartments with a roommate. At the very least, however, your baby should have her own crib. Under no circumstances—ever—should your baby be sleeping with you.

I was told this as a new mom but ignored the advice. I thought my baby was precious and adorable and that cuddling with him at night was the sweetest thing. The fact that he woke up several times a night just made me that much more convinced that allowing him to sleep with me and just rolling over to feed him was best. I was young, naive, and wrong. One night I drifted off to sleep only to wake up to a loud "plop" and a screaming baby. To my horror, I realized that I had inadvertently fallen asleep and pushed my little one off the bed. I was embarrassed and thought I would never forgive myself.

The reality is that having my baby fall on the floor was the least of my worries. Babies die too often from sleeping with a parent who—exhausted and hard-sleeping—simply rolls over and suffocates her own child. It is horrible. Imagine the guilt that these parents must feel. Please do not sleep with your children.

Many studies support the "cry out" method as a viable way to train a baby to sleep through the night. Studies also continue to advise against co-sleeping. Despite the studies, however, some still argue that co-sleeping is acceptable and that the cry-out method is cruel. Although there are studies to support both positions on the issue, use commonsense here and you will see that training your baby to sleep through the night, alone, is in the best interests of both you and your baby.

It is important that you, as a single parent, understand that your reality is different. You do not have the luxury that some co-parenting couples enjoy, in that you cannot alternate sleeping methods, responsibilities, or feeding schedules with the other parent.

Take it from a former single mom who was just as exhausted as you probably are today. The risks of co-sleeping and not teaching your baby to sleep through the night far exceeds any benefit you would get from having your little one sleep with you. I recommend avoiding it at all costs. (This method works only when there is not an extenuating circumstance, such as a health problem with your baby. Please consult a pediatrician or other physician with individual concerns.) Cuddle and snuggle all you want with your little one *before* bed, but then put him or her to bed for the night. There is something to be said for having your bed to yourself, having a little quiet time, and sleeping restfully without a foot in your tummy. This is a boundary, a healthy boundary.

The Importance of Boundaries

As time went on and my children grew, I began to really understand the importance of boundaries. Even during the early stages of development, infants and toddlers desire boundaries. All children desire the gift of structure and protection. Boundaries give children a sense of security. As infants grow, crawl, and eventually walk, it is important that you structure boundaries in such a way that both parent and child can be safe, happy, and comfortable. Children want consistency from their parents. You will find that as you establish consistent boundaries during your children's younger years, the adjustment (and I do mean, major adjustment) to pre-adolescent and teenage years will be easier.

So what do I mean by boundaries? Simply put, I mean rules. I am referring to establishing parameters that are ideal for your child, your home, and your situation. For example, as a toddler ages the need for "individual play time" increases. This is a time when the child plays alone in his bedroom or playpen, while you carry on with day-to-day tasks. Again, this is something I learned over time.

Beginning in toddlerhood my children began to look forward to and appreciate having some alone time (and Mom sure did like it, too!). I go back to single parenting here. You cannot work a full-time job, balance daily chores, oversee finances, and so much more, and then be expected to watch your child every waking second, as they follow you from room to room. It just isn't possible, especially when you have very little help. Do yourself and your precious children a big favor and begin to establish boundaries.

Now, I know some parents are reading this advice and thinking, "I have a 12-year-old and I did not do a very good job setting forth rules when she was younger. What do I do now?" The good news is that *it is never too late* to set boundaries. Whether you are parenting a 5-year-old, 11-year-old, or 16-year-old, know that your child wants instruction. Now your teenager, of course, is not going to readily admit that he wants boundaries. But be sure that he wants them nonetheless.

Single parents, make no apologies here. Set forth rules in your home. Period. No excuses. I realize we are in a day and time of "anything goes," "if it feels good do it," and "to each his own," but that is contrary to God's word. We are in an all-out war for our children's futures. We are in a single-parenting crisis that statistics predict will dictate your child's future. Do not dare allow your child to become just another statistic.

Your Heavenly Father is far above any number written on a sheet of paper. But His word is clear. He challenges, instructs, and commands us to raise up our children in the way they should go, not in the way the world teaches, not in the way that others say is "the new thing." The non-negotiables of your home are those things that you feel strongly about from a biblical parenting perspective. These things never change. As your children, from their earliest years, see that Mom will never change her stance on lying, stealing, cheating, premarital sex, and other issues, they will have the comfort of knowing Mom's predictability and what to expect. They will know—and respect—her boundaries.

Age-Appropriate Rules: Pre-Teen & Adolescent Years

Once you understand the importance of setting boundaries, it is just as important to establish age-appropriate rules. The absolutely hardest thing I have learned during my parenting journey has been the art of letting go. What worked when my children were seven and nine doesn't work when they become 15 and 17. May I be honest? When my son turned about 13 years old, I thought he was the devil incarnate! I mean, my sweet, obedient angel turned into an enraged, argumentative, rude kid. I thought I would pull my hair out. Here I was, in full-time ministry, instructing mothers globally how to parent their children, and my teenager was tearing our house apart.

I have often said that in the earlier years of ministry, when I was teaching parenting classes in my home (while my children were still pre-teens), God had a major sense of humor. He probably smiled down from on high as I taught teen moms how to love on their babies, knowing full-well that my whole world would be turned upside down in just a few years. And then I would really learn what parenting was all about!

You see, no one had adequately prepared me for the pre-teen and teen years. Sure, I had read parenting books on teens and pre-teens. But I do not think that I fully comprehended the magnitude of hormones, maturity, and exercising independence that is natural at that stage of a child's development.

I remember talking to a girlfriend one Sunday after a particularly rough evening with my son. I was in tears over the difficulties I was experiencing. Her son was about a year younger than my son, and I asked her if she was experiencing a similar problem in her home. She replied, "No, but I will be praying for you guys." I walked away from that conversation completely deflated. I was convinced that I was a failure as a parent, that my son was going down the wrong road, and that we were far from normal. I was beyond embarrassed.

Fast forward two years. That same friend called me one day and said, "Help me! I am about to kill my kid!" She began to unload the details of temper tantrums, rage, and disobedience that closely mirrored what I had endured with my own son just a few months earlier. Having finally come to the back end of this whole thing, I was then able to assure her that her journey was completely normal.

Moms of teens, this one is for you. The transition from childhood to adulthood is extremely difficult. Not only does a teenager experience the natural evolution of hormones, body growth, and development, but they naturally begin to question everything they once knew. They are not quite adults, but no longer children. They do not want to be treated as children. They begin to question their spirituality, who God is, if He exists, the boundaries you set forth, and everything in between.

I admit that I did not handle the transition well with my own children, at first. I just could not believe that my son was a teenager. I could not believe that he did not want to spend every waking moment with me, as he once had. He wanted to be with friends. He did not do exactly what I told him to do when I told him to do it. He questioned why I was a single parent and the poor choices I had made in my own past. It is important to note that even though I was living my life for the Lord at this point and had since married, my son was still harboring hurt and anger over my past mistakes. This is a common hurdle that single parents have to jump over that other parents will never know.

You will quite possibly endure your children's anger over a lost father figure in their lives through death, divorce, or absentee parent. You may even (and most likely will) receive the brunt of misplaced anger. How you handle that anger will be crucial to the future health of your relationship with your teen and young adult.

There were a few things I had to learn as my children aged beyond the pre-adolescent years and here they are:

- ***Their* mistakes do not always reflect *your* poor parenting.** Far too often, parents are beating themselves up because ... Pat got arrested. Pat cheated on a test. Pat drove the car without permission. Not every mistake your child makes is proof-positive that you have failed as a parent, so do not internalize it as such. Isn't that true of our relationship with our Heavenly Father? How many times do we fail our Lord? He is certainly not questioning, "What did *I* do wrong?" This is not to say that there are not cases when you have mishandled your parenting duties. There are. We all make mistakes in that regard. But it is vital to your parenting health that you balance your disappointments with your victories. Spending too much time reflecting on where you went wrong every time your child makes a mistake will be to your detriment (and ultimately theirs).

- **They *will* make mistakes.** Embrace it. Understand it. Relish the fact that you would rather have them make mistakes at 13 than at 30. Because I had such a tumultuous childhood (and the added pressure of being a ministry leader), I put way too much pressure on myself to have perfect children. I ruled with an iron fist. I was determined that they would be straight-A students, the best athletes on the team, homecoming court, class representative, and anything else that came their way. They *would* over-achieve. It was some twisted way of showing others that my children would not become a statistic, that they would not become what I once was. It was an internal war that I had to eventually wash in the blood of Jesus. I was not forgiving myself for my own mistakes and past. Therefore, my children had to pay. Once I had forgiven myself, released perfectionism, and embraced my children's mistakes as "normal" learning opportunities, I experienced freedom beyond measure. And you will, too.

- **Relinquishing control of your child's life gives them freedom to make choices.** And good or bad, they learn from the choices. It is healthy to let go. As a Type-A controlling perfectionist, I have to admit this has been a hard one for me. I was the parent who "helped" my kids with all their homework and projects for years. I did everything just shy of putting my name on them! I mean, *I had to*. What would happen if they got a "B" or, heaven forbid, a "C" on their assignments. Parents, I spent years micro-managing every second of my kids' lives. Their rooms had to be beyond spotless, closets organized, and homework completed to perfection. I logged into their school's computer system daily for assignments to ensure that they were completing them properly. It was driving me crazy! And what's worse, it was driving my children crazy! During this time, I talked with a parent who apparently was doing the same thing. She actually made the comment, "I guess I will have to go to college with my son in order to ensure that he maintains good grades." At the time, I rationalized that her comment meant that I was indeed "normal."

Today, however, I see it as the radical, ill-advised statement that it is. Our job in life is to raise our children to be independent, God-fearing, thriving citizens who love the Lord their God and serve Him all the days of their lives. That's it. That's our job. It is not to impress everyone else with the perfect kid we reared. It is not to have him or her become a cookie-cutter image of what we deem as perfection. It is to raise them up to be all God intended for them to be. It is not so that we can live vicariously through them.

Teenager-hood is merely a season. One day, they will grow up, leave your home, and you will be best friends who go have coffee together... (or so I keep hearing).

REFLECTIONS ON CHAPTER 5

HEALTHY BOUNDARIES

1. Why is it important for our children to have boundaries?

_____

_____

_____

_____

_____

2. Do you believe you have established healthy boundaries in your parenting thus far? Why or why not? What are some things you may need to change?

_____

_____

_____

3. What are some non-negotiables of your home?

_____

_____

_____

_____

4. Your children's mistakes do not always reflect your poor parenting. How does that make you feel?

_____

_____

_____

5. Have you struggled with perfectionism or control in your parenting? If so, what can you do about it?

_____

_____

_____

_____

_____

_____

_____

_____

_____

_____

_____

_____

_____

_____

_____

_____

CHAPTER 6

ENCOURAGEMENT

"When you go through deep waters, I will be with you.
When you go through rivers of difficulty, you will not drown."
(Isaiah 43:2)

There are days when I feel like a complete failure as a parent. I am tired, confused, overwhelmed, and, if I am being completely honest, simply do not want to do it any more. I want to scream, "Am I doing anything right? Throw me some encouragement, Lord!" Sometimes you just need an *atta-girl*.

The Bible is full of such encouragement. I am going to go out on a limb here and believe that at least one of you has felt the same as me—as though you were wandering through a parenting desert unsure if you were doing it correctly. Let me give you a minute to decide if that's you. Good. There you are! So now there are two of us who aren't convinced that we are perfect parents. The truth is, I don't know that any of us hasn't felt ill-equipped in our parenting skills at some point along the way. Thankfully, our Heavenly Father has given us such great encouragement to remind us that *He* is well-equipped.

It is common for all parents, married or not, to feel as though they are alone on their journey. Satan is a mastermind at whispering to us that no one else cares about our children (even when we have a loving spouse), that the weight of the world falls on our shoulders alone, and that we will never be able to raise successful children. This is especially true of single parents. As you lie awake at night, recapping your day and dreaming of bright futures for your children, there is no one to share those thoughts with. It can be a lonely place. When you feel that you are on this parenting journey all alone, know that the Creator of your children, the One who knew them in your womb, is with you.

"Be strong and courageous! Do not be afraid and do not panic before them. For the Lord your God will personally go ahead of you. He will never fail you nor abandon you."
(Deuteronomy 31:6)

"This is my command—be strong and courageous! Do not be afraid or discouraged. For the Lord your God is with you wherever you go." (Joshua 1:9)

"Do not be afraid for I am with you." (Isaiah 43:5a)

The Lord promises never to leave us. It is important that we understand this simple truth—even when we don't feel as though He is around. He is. Our heart can be so deceitful. It plays tricks on us. (Remember Jeremiah 17:9?) We cannot live our lives, nor parent our children, convinced that the Lord is only with us when we *feel* Him.

Trusting God with Your Present

Our family went through a particularly tough 12 months recently, and I was almost at my breaking point. I was running a fast-growing nonprofit organization, parenting three children, and trying desperately to manage the many demands in my life. It seemed that everything that could go wrong had gone wrong. My children had battled major physical problems. Our finances were interesting, to say the least. The ministry presented a whole new set of challenges. I found myself in tears every day for weeks. I had taken a little time off work to be with my family, but all I could do was cry. I could not wait for the children to leave for school so that I could sit on the sofa and cry. I prayed and cried (probably crying more than praying). I could not understand why I was having to walk through the difficulties of our circumstances. "Lord, I've had my share of heartaches and disappointments already in my life. I'm at my quota! Why me, Lord?!" I would plead. After weeks of hosting my pity party, I felt the Lord whispering to me in my heart.

"I will never leave you. I have not abandoned you. I am with you."

It was music to my ears. Never before had that scripture come alive the way it did in that moment. It wasn't that I did not know that in my head. I have been a Christian for many years. But in that moment, in that season of my life, I needed to know that my Savior saw me crying out to Him. He saw my tears.

I needed to be reminded that although I may not understand all the steps on *how* it will work out, it will indeed work out. Many of you are in that place today, right now, as you read. You feel completely and utterly alone. You feel that you have not only been abandoned by a helpmate but by the very Creator of your soul.

Although I cannot explain to you the "whys" of your life, I know that God loves you. Beyond all else, He loves each of us and desires intimacy with us. He will never abandon us. I have learned that through those years when I felt "abandoned," the Lord was teaching me great strength. He was teaching me what it was to parent with courage. He was teaching me the love He has for me in a deeper way. I once heard Evangelist Perry Stone say, "Many of you think the Lord has forgotten you, but don't you know that the Teacher never talks during the test?" Amen!

The pressures of managing a budget, parenting children, and balancing employment, friendships, church life, and more can crack even the most experienced parent. It is during those times when I am near "cracking" (such as my crying pity party) that I go to my all-time favorite scripture:

> "*When you go through deep waters, I will be with you. When you go through rivers of difficulty, you will not drown. When you walk through the fire of oppression, you will not be burned up; the flames will not consume you. For I am the Lord, your God, the Holy One of Israel, your Savior.*" *(Isaiah 43:2-3a)*

Doesn't that give you chills? I love how the Lord speaks so plainly to His people. He wants us to know that He loves us. He wants us to understand that our temporary hardship does not reflect the future joy He has promised us. We are safe in His arms. And yes, I know some of you may be thinking, "Temporary? This certainly does not seem temporary! I have been struggling financially for eight years. I have parented alone for 10 years." Abraham was over 100 when God began fulfilling the promise to make him father of many nations. Sarah was in her eighties. I don't know about you, but after I reached about 42, I would have been certain that God had forgotten about me. He who has promised is faithful! He has promised us that He will not leave us. You are not alone.

Trusting God with Your Past

Perhaps you fear that your past mistakes have somehow ruined your children. Maybe your children have seen and heard too much. Maybe you once exposed your children to a different lifestyle. Maybe you have made some colossal mistakes. I know I sure have! You must first free yourself from the guilt of your past life. The Bible says that once we are saved we are all new creations in Christ.

We all have a past. The really good news is that the Lord has forgiven us of those sins and cast them as far as the east is from the west. He wants you to have a new beginning. The Lord is quick to forgive us, yet we sometimes cannot forgive ourselves. You must let go of any mistake you have made. There is *no* condemnation in Christ Jesus. The shame, embarrassment, and guilt you carry is, again, a lie from the enemy that keeps you bound and discouraged. You are complete in Christ Jesus. There is nothing lacking in your life now that you know Him. Embrace that truth.

In my early years of parenting, I was living an entirely different lifestyle. As very young toddlers, my children saw and heard screaming, profanity, abuse, and destruction. When I committed my life to the Lord, I was crushed when I thought of all that my children had seen. I had duplicated much of my own childhood into my children's lives. I was ashamed and felt as though I had failed my children. How could they ever turn out to be more than me? What if they made the same mistakes I did?

In Proverbs 22:6 we are called to "raise up our children in the way they should go" so that when they are older they will not depart from it. We are not promised that we will do so flawlessly. What do we, as humans, ever do flawlessly? We are imperfect and sinful. You have made mistakes along the way, and you will make more. I am sure of it. Nonetheless, our children can still grow up to be all God intended them to be. They can still flourish despite our own failures as parents. His adequacy far exceeds our inadequacies. As we raise them up in the ways of the Lord, His grace covers all those areas in which we are still learning.

I am on the back end of this parenting journey (at least parenting them in my home) and I could not be more proud of how my children are turning out. For every lie the enemy whispered in my ear, God has interceded. My own love for my children and His love for us all has covered a multitude of sins.

Trusting God with Your Worries and Fear

Fear and worry were other areas that often paralyzed my parenting abilities. I constantly worried that my children would make the same mistakes I had ... or even worse. What sometimes started as a legitimate concern would in time evolve into a full-fledged panic attack. If my children were late calling me, I worried that they were not where they said they were. If they scored poorly on a test, I worried they would forever live in government housing on government assistance. *What if my children have a baby outside marriage? What if they drink and drive? What if they get married too soon? What if they never marry? What if my children never have a father who loves them?* Fear consumed me. Worry inundated my thoughts.

For every time you have worried financially that you would not have enough, our Father says He will supply all our needs.

For every time you have worried that your children would not have a father to love them and that they would somehow suffer eternally from that loss, our Father promises to be a father to the fatherless.

For every tear you have cried, He heard you, bottled it, and promised to be close to your broken heart.

For every time you worried that there was no way on earth it would work out, He says that all things will work for your good.

For every time you worried that you would forever be alone, His word promises to put the lonely in families.

For every time you were weak, He promised to be strong.

For every time you feared lack, He provided.

When we are in the midst of our valley, it does not seem to matter to us whether we are going to learn something from this trial. We do not care that we may one day help encourage another on that same path. We simply want out. We want the Lord to reach down, pluck us out of our situation, and shake His finger at all those who hurt us along the way. But in my valleys of parenting I have learned the most about myself. In my quiet times, alone with the Lord, when I was able to confess my fears to Him repeatedly and always. And from that simple confession He would proclaim newness over my life and my situation, and there would be peace.

"For I am about to do something new. I have already begun.
Do you not see it? I will make a pathway in the wilderness.
I will create rivers in dry wasteland." (Isaiah 43:19)

Our Heavenly Father has a way of taking our mess and developing a full-fledged message for others. He has a way of working out things for our good and giving us far more than we could have ever prayed for, asked, or imagined. His plans for our children's lives are far better than we could ever orchestrate. Imagine this. He loves our children more than we do! Can you even imagine it? Relinquish the worry that you are carrying regarding your children's future. Even if they make some mistakes (and we both know they will), God has him right in the palm of His hand.

Lastly, I want to challenge each of you to lay down the burdens of this world. Many of you are attempting to carry far more than you ever could. The Lord promises in Matthew 11:30 that His yoke is easy and His burden is light. Cast the cares of this world upon Him. Isn't it funny how we say that we "gave it to the Lord" when the truth is that we never actually did? One day a friend held me accountable in this very area. I was going through a challenging circumstance in my life and would frequently say (all holy and such), "I've just given it to the Lord. There's nothing more I can do about it. I'm just giving it to Him."

After conversation number 132 about this particular problem (that I had already given to the Lord), my friend asked, "If you have really given it to the Lord, why do you feel the constant need to talk about it?" Well, after the smoke cleared from my fury that she dare question my deep spirituality, I thought about what she had just asked. She went on to explain that many Christians give something to the Lord only to constantly take it back.

It is like walking down a road carrying five heavy sacks of grain. A friend has agreed to come along, and he is driving a truck. He has offered multiple times to drive both the grain and us, but we decide to go it alone. We just need him to drive alongside for good conversation, we explain. We do all right, at first. As the journey wears on, however, beads of sweat surface on our heads. Although the trip becomes progressively more difficult, we insist on carrying the load. We drop sacks down to our waist, and eventually we can barely drag the sacks behind us. And even then, it is difficult for us to accept help. The same is true in our spiritual lives.

The Lord is not simply coming along as a good conversationalist. He wants to carry our load. It is easy for Him. He has a super-sized God truck that we don't have. He can carry multiple loads. Yet we are, in our own strength, trying to drag the five grain sacks with us. Stop dragging the sacks! They are heavy. You are weak without the truck. We all need the truck.

REFLECTIONS ON CHAPTER 6

ENCOURAGEMENT

1. Have you ever reached a point in your parenting when you were at your wit's end? Describe it.

   _____

   _____

   _____

   _____

2. Have you ever been convinced that you were all alone and no one else cared?

   _____

   _____

3. Write Joshua 1:9 here as a constant reminder of God's promise.

   _____

   _____

   _____

   _____

   _____

4. What is the most difficult challenge you face as a single parent? What scripture have you chosen to cling to?

   _____

   _____

5. Has there been a time when someone in your family, church, or a close friend has given especially kind words of encouragement? If so, write them here. If not, write down what you would have liked to hear, so that you may one day share the words of encouragement with another.

_____

_____

_____

_____

6. What is a past mistake you have made that you fear affects your children?

_____

_____

_____

_____

7. What does 2 Corinthians 5:17 say?

_____

_____

_____

_____

8. What load have you carried on your own that you were never intended to carry?

_____

_____

_____

_____

_____

9. What is one lie that the enemy has whispered in your ear about your parenting abilities?

_____

_____

_____

_____

_____

10. Think of a time when God has provided in your time of emotional need. What did He do?

_____

_____

_____

_____

11. Read Isaiah 43:19. What is the "new" thing you are believing God for as a parent? As a child of God?

_____

CHAPTER 7

THE FOUR C's

"The four C's are those keys that I believe are crucial in parenting your children to live the God-intended dream."

N
o, no, no. Not color, cut, clarity, and carat. But we *are* talking diamonds, here. That is exactly what our children are. They are rare diamonds given to us by the Lord to mold and shape into all that He intended them to be. It is a great honor and a great responsibility. The four C's are those keys that I believe are crucial in parenting your children to live the God-intended dream.

Communication

From the time our children are formed in the womb to the time we part ways on our death bed, communication is vital to a healthy long-term relationship. Parenting studies suggest that at as early as 26 weeks gestation, many babies can already recognize their mother's voice. According to Kim O'Neill, author of *Bond With Your Baby Before Birth,* the months prior to your child's birth are crucial to developing a strong mother-baby bond. Playing music for the baby, reading, and talking are all said to help the baby make sense of the new world around her once she is born. In addition, brain function development is enhanced, and family bonds are formed. There are even studies that suggest that your child's academic performance can be enhanced by early in-womb communication.

Your child's need for communication with his parents does not disintegrate when he is two, 12, or 25. Someone is always talking to your children, telling them what to do, who to become, and what type of future to lead. Make sure it is *you*. The Child Development Institute suggests that great conversation is the catalyst for any future relationship between parent and child.

My dad was born in 1935 during a time when most men did not share their emotions freely—and certainly not with their children. Because my mother had died when I was very young and my dad detested genuine conversation, I often felt that I had no one to talk to. Most assuredly, this contributed at least in part to my poor decision-making during my teen years.

You must talk to your baby, talk to your toddler, your 10-year old, your teen. It never grows old. They never become too old. Ensure that you spend time with your children every day, no matter their age, and that that time is quality. Learn who they are, what they like, their hopes and dreams. Watch them grow. I realize that I am speaking to parents with children of all ages and, consequently, questions will arise. Moms of toddlers, you may feel that conversation is meaningless at such an early age. Again, I would submit to you that not only do numerous studies support early communication as vital for your child's academic performance, cognitive skills, and language development, but your toddler loves the sound of your voice. He wants to hear you sing to him, talk to him, teach him. If you start this trend early on, they look to you for guidance in future learning stages, too.

Talking to Teens

Moms of teenagers, you may worry that because you did not develop early communication with your teen, it is somehow too late for you now. It absolutely is not! Start now. I know this is no easy feat. I have two teenagers. I realize that it sometimes seems they live on another planet from the rest of us. Do you remember what it was like to be a teenager? We vow that we will never be like our parents who were completely disconnected from reality when we were teenagers, but somehow we fall into the same parenting rut. We are convinced that our teens will never listen to us and they are convinced that all parents have secret pacts to ruin their lives.

Talk *to* your teen. Do not talk *at* your teen. You will soon learn that this is an art that requires some creativity. Avoid closed-end questions or the conversation may go something like this:

"How was your day, honey?"

"Fine."

"Did anything interesting happen?"

"No."

"Did you have that test in history class?"

"Yes."

"How did you do?"

"Fine. May I go to my room?"

The end. Not quite as successful as you may have imagined, huh? You're the parent. You're the adequately-equipped, well-diversified, highly-creative communicator, so take this conversation a different route. Learn to navigate the tricky waters of "huh" and "yeah" and hit your teen with the art of surprise.

"Guess what I did today!" you may say on the drive home from school.

"Huh?" (He's wondering why you would think he would care what you did today.)

"I booked two new clients to the Davis account! I'm so excited! What do ya think about that?"

"Uh. That's great, Mom. What's for dinner?"

"Well, my great day put me in a great mood. I'll cook whatever you want, but you have to tell me the very best thing that happened to you today, first."

"What?! I don't feel like it. Forget it. I'll just eat *whatever*."

"Oh, good, whatever happens to brussel sprouts and spinach."

"Uh, wait, uh. Let me think. The best thing that happened to me...."

And there it is, parents. A simple conversation where you have not invited your teen to participate in the Spanish Inquisition, but rather to enjoy a casual conversation with his parent. (Granted, at first, you may be the only one enjoying the conversation, but they will come around.) Do not give up after the first or second or tenth try. Keep at it. Be persistent. Countless times my own teens have given me the one-word utterance in response to my efforts to launch into meaningful conversations, but persistence is key.

The more I persist, the quicker they break down! Teens are no different from the rest of us. They want to know they are understood, that someone cares about their ideas, and that they have value. Isn't that what we all want? Even the most angry teens desire to feel valued. He may have gone far too long without feeling valued and has consequently become angry, rude, and distant.

I am not minimizing the difficulties that lie ahead when attempting to break down years of pent-up anger with a preteen or teen. I know it is there. I have seen it with my own children and many, many others. But just as our Heavenly Father never grows tired of extending His love and compassion to us, lovingly ushering us into a relationship with Him, we should never grow tired of doing the same thing with our own children.

Consistency

A parent who remains consistent maintains success. In my own childhood, I remember having anxiety riding home on the bus, not knowing the parent I would get for that evening. Would I get the happy, jovial Dad who would joke with us as we ate dinner and recapped our day? Or would I get the raging alcoholic who destroyed the house and cussed like a sailor? Or would I get someone in between? It was a daily concern. Children desire consistency.

They need to know that they have a parent who cares enough to ensure they have a routine. It gives them something to count on. When a child has gone through a divorce or lives daily with the absence of a second parent, her world has been turned upside down. It is traumatic. How you navigate the rough waters of divorce, death, or absentee parent will help guide your child with an adequate coping ability and even deeper understanding of his Heavenly Father's love.

Children need to know what to expect, day in and day out. They need to know that they are not coming home to World War III because Mom had a bad day at work. Along the same lines, they must know that your implementation of discipline is not contingent upon your day at work, the behavior of your ex-spouse, or your financial status. They must know that, as a parent, you are committed to continual learning on their behalf and you will do everything in your power to ensure their safety, comfort, and security. You will teach them through rules and boundaries. You will implement an appropriate punishment when boundaries have been crossed. End of story.

Mom, having a bad day does not excuse poor or ineffective parenting. Routine and consistency are your best friends in effective parenting. Your baby is safe. Your toddler feels comfortable.

And whether he likes it or not, your teen knows exactly what to expect. Dependability teaches integrity to your child. Of course, there are surprise ice cream outings and occasional exceptions, but as a general rule, very little should change.

Clarity

This one is most important as your child ages. While the 3-year-old may not require an explanation on why it is important not to touch the stove, your 13-year-old will surely want to know why she cannot spend the night at Mandy's house. I did not understand this during my older children's preteen years. I saw it as a form of disobedience when they questioned my response. They were to do what I told them to do. Period. No ifs, ands, or buts. What I deemed as disobedience, however, was actually independence and there is a *big* difference.

We all know those adults who will not leave their parents' house or who continually transition back into their parents' home as an adult. None of us want *that* to be our children. I know there are exceptions to every rule, but in general, many adults who cannot seem to find that sustainable independence as an adult failed to learn independence as a teen. It is important that we foster an environment where our growing preteens and teens know that they can ask for clarity about our decisions without it being deemed "questioning" our authority.

Constantly evaluate your responses to your children as they age. Do take the time to consider fair requests to spend time with friends, have sleepovers, and the like. Be sure that you are responding to requests in an age-appropriate way and taking the time to recognize their maturity. Our job as a parent is not to do everything for them but to effectively equip them to navigate life on their own. This aging process comes with maturity and privileges. Don't be a "helicopter mom," hovering over your child's every activity, determined to bully them into submission, controlling every aspect of their lives, and ignoring their rising age.

Offer the "whys" of your denials and use them as teaching opportunities. Your child may not agree with you, but at least he will know that you value him enough to explain how and why you arrived at your response.

Christianity

The number one way we all parent efficiently and effectively is our walk with the Lord. Nothing, not one thing, can replace our daily time with Him. The strength we gather from His word and the truth of His teachings is invaluable. Do not proclaim that you do not have the time to spend in devotion daily with the Lord. You cannot afford not to. This is not to say that this is some legalistic ritual but rather a genuine heart-felt prayer time, where you can cast all your burdens on Him and give Him the praise He is due.

Many times through the years I have been at an absolute loss for what to do or say next regarding my own children. I simply did not have the storybook answer that others seemed to. No matter how many parenting books I read, there always seemed to be something in my life that was an exception to the rule. I simply did not have all the answers and did not seem able to find them. That is when I turned to prayer. I fell to my knees and cried out to God Most High. I cried tears of frustration and anger when my children had disappointed me. I prayed in thanksgiving when they chose wisely. I prayed over my children before bed. I prayed over their bedrooms and cars when they weren't home. I prayed with them before school. I prayed when I spanked them. I prayed as I wrote them letters. I prayed as I talked to them about heavy issues.

And then … I prayed some more.

I could list countless examples of my failures as a parent. I felt like I was doing the whole thing wrong. I mourned when I had made poor decisions or exemplified wrong behavior. But I clung to the truth of the Word when all else seemed to have failed me. My walk with the Lord has ensured my survival. It has not been an added burden, an added pressure that I put upon myself. Rather, it has been the strength that has sustained me, the grace that has cleansed me, and the love that has pursued me.

You cannot do this parenting thing without your Heavenly Father. And I don't mean some fly-by-night, on-again, off-again, call-on-my-genie type of relationship. I mean, you recognize that the Lord God Almighty gave you these precious diamonds for a reason. He blessed you with this gift of life. He is not surprised by your circumstances. He is not confused about your future or worried that you will somehow fail. He is your rock, your source, your strength, your redeemer, your savior, your counselor, your physician, and your should-be best friend.

REFLECTIONS on CHAPTER 7

THE FOUR C's

1. How do you feel the lines of communication flow currently with your child?

_____

_____

_____

_____

_____

2. What can you do better?

_____

_____

_____

_____

3. What time of day is easiest for you to begin intentional conversation with your child? What types of things can you discuss? Think of some age-appropriate conversation starters.

_____

_____

_____

_____

4. A parent who maintains consistency maintains success. What does this mean to you? Give an example.

_____

_____

_____

5. Do bad days affect your parenting? How can you avoid "moody" parenting?

_____

_____

_____

_____

_____

6. Give an example of a rule appropriate for a 5-year-old but not appropriate for a 10-year-old.

_____

_____

_____

_____

7. Have you displayed rigidity or flexibility in your parenting style? Which do you think is better and why?

_____

_____

_____

_____

8. Have you viewed your child's desire for more information as disobedience or a healthy progression of his maturity and independence?

_____

_____

_____

_____

_____

9. Consider any rule in your house that may need adjustment based on your child's age progression (either currently or in the future).

_____

_____

_____

_____

_____

10. Your daily time with the Lord is your number one parenting tool. When do you have time with Him? Why is it important to do so?

_____

_____

_____

_____

_____

CHAPTER 8

BIBLE BASICS

*" Some of us are not maximizing all the fullness of the life
that God has for us while here on earth because we
choose not to tap into these basic principles...."*

As we finish our journey together, I wanted to address three major Biblical principles that I have not touched upon yet, but that I believe are critical not only in raising Christian men and women but also in just having all-around good citizens—-contributors to society. Some of us are not maximizing all the fullness of the life that God has for us while here on earth because we choose not to tap into these basic principles.

You will find that all three principles are dying arts that some would deem "old fashioned" or "outmoded." Since I am using verses straight from the word of God and it never grows out-of-date, I pray that He will change a few minds.

Principle #1 - Servanthood

*"So he (Jesus) got up from the table, took off his robe,
wrapped a towel around his waist, and poured water into
a basin. Then he began to wash the disciples' feet, drying*

> *them with the towel he had around him."*
> *(John 13:4-5)*

Let me set the scene for you. The disciples had been on an amazing journey with the Lord Jesus. They had seen Him heal the blind, raise the dead, turn water into wine, deliver sermons beyond anything they had ever heard, and hold to account the religious leaders of the day. The disciples had grown to love Jesus very much. And the scriptures says in verse 1 of the same chapter that Jesus loved them, as well. And here, at the end of his ministry, as His own death drew near, He pauses to teach the disciples a valuable lesson of what it is to serve and love one another.

Why do you suppose Jesus chose this moment to wash the disciples' feet? I mean, He had been with them for years. He was teaching them all sorts of things. Why now? I believe that the significance of this moment is elevated even more by His timing. He wanted the disciples' attention. He had taken time to develop relationships with each one. He wanted them to truly hear what He was saying and see His teaching in action.

He not only spoke of the significance of this moment, but He put His words into action. Imagine the silence around the room. Imagine what they must have thought as each anxiously awaited the presence of the Savior at their feet. Their Savior, the King, the Lamb of God, was washing their feet! It must have been a sight to behold.

The beauty of this scene is not lost on me. Servanthood should never be about obligation but rather should grow out of the richness of your relationship with your Lord Jesus. It is from the gratitude of all the Lord has already done that we look to serve others. We recognize that no matter how bad we have it, there is always someone worse off. We recognize that every good thing that we have comes from the Lord, and we desire to honor Him by displaying that same spirit of servanthood for others.

This is especially important with our children. Let's be honest. We live in a day and age when its-all-about-me and what's-in-it-for-me attitudes. The self-absorption of many of our youth (and adults, too) has reached an all-time high. We are more concerned about how much stuff we can accumulate than how much we can give away. We pay more attention to our luxury cars than to our elderly. We are more concerned with sitting in our same spot on Sundays than with who may be missing from the pews that we could invite.

When is the last time you asked, "What is it that I can do today to serve others?" Have you looked around for those less fortunate or those who simply need a touch from heaven. God works through people. You are the one He works through.

Children must understand early that the world does not revolve around them. Teach them to think of others first. Nothing warms my heart more than to go on an outreach to a local nursing home or hospital and see single mothers whom I minister to locally there at the hospital early with their three children in tow. They are setting the precedent of servanthood in their home. Serving gives us perspective on our own problems. It gives us value. It gives the Lord an opportunity to use us. And it teaches our children to avoid selfish behavior.

It is also important to make a distinction here between servanthood and chores. Your children should absolutely, unequivocally, have chores that you expect them to complete. Chores are part of being on the family team. We all have tasks to complete to keep the family running smoothly. Cleaning their room, dishes, washing clothes, sweeping, mopping, dusting, taking out the trash, and bathroom duty are just a few examples of things our children can help us do. But their daily family obligations are not in lieu of teaching them about serving others. Chores become service when our children take the initiative to take out the trash when it isn't their job for the week or when they fold clothes without being asked. When this happens, we can stand proudly with an ear-to-ear grin knowing that they finally "get it."

For more ideas on serving others, I highly recommend Dino Rizzo's book *Servolution* (Zondervan).

Principle #2 - Living a Life of Excellence

"Work willingly at everything you do, as though you were working for the Lord rather than for people."
(Colossians 3:23)

I have repeatedly told my children that the most important thing for me as a mother is to see them grow in their relationship with the Lord. And I have tried to keep that my focus as I parent. As you know, I have struggled with perfectionism in the past—worrying that my kids must be perfect in academics, athletics, social events, and more. As the Lord has revealed this to me and I have worked to move past it, my bright, coy teenagers have been very creative in attempting to manipulate my new-found freedom.

Just because I have decided that academics aren't everything and that my children will probably not be valedictorians of their graduating class does not mean that academics are nothing. I still expect a level of excellence in academic performance in my home, much to the chagrin of my teenage son.

"But Mom, I thought you said the most important thing is my relationship with God," he may say. And he's right. The Bible, however, challenges us to do everything as unto to the Lord.

The verse speaks of doing everything with excellence, living our lives with excellence. Grades are not the have-all and end-all of life.

Now I know I may ruffle a few feathers with that statement, especially for those of you who are fighting regularly with your children about homework and assignments. But let me clarify. There was a time in my life when grades defined me. I was a straight-A student who served as class president and earned valedictory honors. No matter how out of control my home life was, I could always count on my grades. The Lord gifted me with a bright mind, good study habits, and organizational skills and I was grateful. It was the one way that I knew I could always please my earthly daddy. Consequently, my good grades allowed me to convince myself the he had a deeper love for me.

As I became a parent and my children got older, I saw that in some ways I was transferring this same parenting style to my own children. I placed emphasis on grades beyond all else. It was A's and B's all the way, and anything less was unacceptable. After all, my children were bright! I saw, however, that my desire to be perfect (and thus my desire for my children also to be perfect) led me to parent poorly. It wasn't enough for my children to enter the Science Fair. They had to win it.

It wasn't enough for them to get a B on a test. They had to be the high-scorer in the class. I helped with projects. Who am I kidding? I *did* the projects and let my children watch! There was a time that if one of my children brought home a C or lower, I was just short of curling onto the bathroom floor in the fetal position and plugging my ears with my fingers. And I am serious! Praise God, He gave me freedom in that area.

Having said all that, grades are still important. They exemplify what our children are learning and their efforts and also reveal potential learning problems in some cases. The most important part of grades is the attitude behind which they are pursued. We teach our children that they are to work "as unto the Lord." Maybe your child's very best is to earn a C on that project. Be okay with that. Challenge him to push hard, research, and be creative. But recognize that his hard-earned C is better than an A earned by a child whose parent actually did all the work!

The same is true in all areas of our life. We display our Christianity through our actions and behaviors far more than through our words. We are to work hard at our employment, as if we are working for the Lord and not that mean-spirited boss. We may be called to be in that job to witness to that very boss. We work with integrity. We show up on time, follow the rules, and remain honest with employees and co-workers. It is simple, really. Yet how often do we see co-workers bad-mouth the boss, consistently show up late to work, and dishonestly adjust pricing for profit? We are to be an example to our children of what it is to work hard for what you have and to do it with the highest level of integrity attainable.

When your child goes to interview at the local fast-food restaurant for potential employment, teach him to wear business slacks, hold his head high, and make eye contact. When he secures the job, teach him about punctuality, professionalism, and efficiency. Do not wait until he has graduated college and begins pursuing a career to teach him basic skills of living a life of excellence.

It starts early and happens often. Teach your 2-year-old about picking up her books and placing them on her bookshelf. Then, as she ages, teach her to do it neatly. Teach her about taking care of those things the Lord has blessed her with and working hard when Mom asks her to do it.

Principle #3 - Manners

"Do unto others as you would have them do unto you."
(Luke 6:31)

The basis of all manners is simply to consider others first. Treat them the way you want to be treated. Ah, the Golden Rule. We were taught it as young children, but oftentimes along the way, it loses its value in our lives. We hear repeatedly that chivalry is dead. Teens roll their eyes at the elderly. Young men do not allow young ladies the first seats. They do not open car doors or any door for that matter. The young do not honor the elderly. Oh, that we would all get back to Bible Basics 101!

Do you want to know the best way to have a lasting relationship with your child? Teach him manners and use those same manners with him. Do you want to know how to have a lasting, productive relationship with a co-worker? Take great care to use your best manners, thinking of how you could serve her first. Interested in pursuing long-term friendships? Be kind. Be thoughtful. Be courteous.

Hold open the door for a stranger. Allow someone to skip you in line. Respond with "please" and "thank you."

Yes, I realize the simplicity of the instruction, but I also realize its significant contribution to our relationships and to that of our children's future.

REFLECTIONS ON CHAPTER 8

BIBLE BASICS

1. Why is it important to teach our children servanthood?

_____

_____

_____

_____

2. What are some ways you and your children can serve others together?

_____

_____

_____

_____

3. What is the difference between perfectionism and living a life "as unto the Lord"?

_____

_____

_____

_____

_____

4. What are some ways you can display Christianity to your children? Do you strive for excellence in your walk with the Lord?

_____

_____

5. What is the value in teaching your children about hard work?

_____

_____

_____

_____

6. What is the Golden Rule? Write it here.

_____

_____

_____

_____

7. Are you teaching your children good manners? Give an example.

_____

_____

_____

_____

_____

_____

_____

_____

_____

A LETTER TO YOU

Dear Precious Parent,

I know there have been times when you felt absolutely certain you would drown under all the pressures in your world. I know you have felt like tossing in the towel. You have been certain that no one could possibly understand your story, and even if they knew it all, they may reject you. You have questioned God, questioned yourself, and felt inadequate for the task at hand. You have feared that your children would not be all they could be or that you would somehow mess everything up.

Please know that there is someone who understands. In fact, there are millions across the country who truly do understand. But more importantly than all of us, your Heavenly Father understands. He has seen all those tears, all those nights of unrest, and all those times you sat alone caring for your children, wondering if He heard your prayers. He heard them. He his waiting for just the perfect time to radically transform your life, so that only He can get all the glory He is due.

He is good, truly good. He is full of grace and mercy and He loves us more than you or I could ever know.

My deepest prayer for you is that you love the Lord your God with all your heart, that you know Him more intimately every day, and that you will seek out a local body of Christ and stay planted there so you can grow in Him.

In Christ,
Jennifer Maggio

Introduction

Our hope in providing you with this leader's guide is that you will have a general direction on how to facilitate small group study. Our intention is not to overwhelm leaders with a multitude of rules, but rather to provide encouragement and direction for your group time. Use this as a guide, knowing that we want to encourage you always to be sensitive to the Holy Spirit and spend more time on each section as needed. Depending on your group, you may spend two or three weeks on each chapter of the book.

Additionally, we recommend that groups have 10 or fewer participants. As you grow to more than 10 members, you may have what is referred to as "large group time" and then divide into smaller groups for further discussion in a small group format.

For more information on how to facilitate an effective Single Moms ministry program purchase *The Single Moms Ministry Resource Kit.*

Week 1: The "I" in Parent

Introduction

Take this time to introduce all single parents in the group. Ask members to share their first thoughts when becoming a parent.

Discussion

☐ Have parents discuss how they feel about parenthood now. Do they still see it as a blessing or a burden?

☐ Ask members to share which question spoke to them most: Am I enjoying my current season? Do I feel good enough—worthy of love? Do I realize that God put a gift inside of me?

☐ It is important to look at ourselves first when parenting. We must evaluate our own struggles, emotional woes, and Spiritual growth. Discuss.

☐ Read Ecclesiastes 3:1 aloud. What does it mean to enjoy your season as a single parent? Discuss ways to embrace your parenting season.

Prayer

Father, help us to recognize our children as the blessings they are. Help us keep perspective on the gifts that You have given and Your powerful hand upon us. Help us that our children look to us as examples of faith, love, and joy. Father, we thank You for Your provision in our lives. Give us wisdom as we parent.

Week 2: The "I" in Parent 2

Introduction

Take a moment to introduce any new members to the rest of the group. Discuss last week's lesson on enjoying your season. Invite members to share anything the Lord has revealed in regard to joyfully embracing their parenting season.

Discussion

☐ Read Isaiah 43:2-3 aloud. What does God promises us?

☐ Ask members to share about their "river of difficulty."

☐ How can the Lord help them overcome it?

☐ What is the dream that God put inside you?

☐ Do you feel worthy enough to achieve it? Have members discuss the reality that God would never give us a dream that we cannot achieve with His guidance in our lives. Foster a discussion on rebuilding dreams and hopes that may have been disrupted by past disappointments.

Prayer Time

In today's prayer time, allow members to pray in groups of 2 or 3. Encourage them to pray aloud for one another and to submit their hopes and dreams to the Lord God.

Week 3: Living as an Example

Introduction

Open up by allowing members to share one fond memory they have from childhood. Follow the fond memory with one trait you admired about your own parent(s).

Discussion

☐ What is one thing your son or daughter does that is "just like you"? Perhaps it is a facial expression or behavior.

☐ Is there something in your life that you are currently doing or have done that you fear your child may duplicate? Allow the members to discuss past hurt and disappointments, as well as confess any area of their lives that may not be honoring the Lord. (Allow extra time here, as needed. It is important that members are able to express the recesses of their heart.)

☐ Ask the group to share the number one way they are committing to raise their children in a godly fashion.

☐ Oftentimes, unbelievers say that Christianity is too hard. There are too many restrictions and guidelines, when all you really want to do is have a good time. Why is it important that we teach our children about sexual immorality and other sins?

sexual purity but the practical ramifications of sexual immorality, such as unplanned pregnancy, disease, emotional brokenness from a failed relationship, and others.

☐ Why does the Bible put restrictions in our lives? (Be sure to note our Heavenly Father's heart to protect us from the danger that lies in sin.)

Prayer

Father, I thank You that Your word says that there is not one sin that could ever separate us from Your love. I thank You that You love us that much. I thank You that You love us even when we seem unlovable to others. I thank You that Your blood washes us white as snow. Father, we believe for our children, right now, that they will not be hindered by our past mistakes. We pray for strength to live a life that is honoring to You and that we may be a living example to our children of Your grace, mercy, and holiness. Amen.

Week 4: Living as an Example 2

Introduction

Open up with a discussion of what it means to be a living example for our children. Ask members to share anything that the Lord may have revealed this week in reference to living a pure life.

Discussion

☐ Give an example of when it was particularly hard in your life to be honest. Were you able to do it?

☐ What are some examples of little "white lies" we tell our chil-

dren or teach our children to tell others?

☐ Read Colossians 3:17, 23 aloud. Discuss the significance of

☐   Ask participants to identify the areas of their parenting style that need improving in relation to the following questions: Am I speaking in a way that honors the Lord? Do I exemplify the heart of Christ? Do I want my children to duplicate my behavior? Do I behave the same both inside and outside my home? Have I taught my children, both through word and action, that a relationship with Jesus is the most important thing? Open up the discussion to allow members to share what areas they struggle in, what they do best in, and how they can continually improve.

Prayer time

Break participants up into groups of two. Allow each prayer partner to pray for each other, specifically asking the Lord for guidance and wisdom in relation to becoming living examples in our children's lives. Encourage them to petition Him for strength for those areas in which they may be weak.

Week 5: Feeding the Green-Eyed Monster

Introduction

Begin by having participants write down one material thing in their lives that they desperately want. It can be either a small or large item, but it must be material. Ask them to write down how often they think about the items.

Discussion

☐ Have members describe the biggest temper tantrum they ever threw as a kid. (A visual description would be a great icebreaker!)

☐   Discuss how it makes you feel when you see disobedient chil-

☐ As a single parent, it is easy to feel guilty for your child's lack of a two-parent home, financial strain, or long work hours. Allow members to discuss this potential guilt and what they have been known to do to overcompensate for the guilt.

☐ Discuss what effect(s) this has on their children.

☐ Is there an area for which any of the participants are struggling to forgive themselves?

☐ Read 1 John 1:9 aloud to the group.

Prayer

Father, we thank You that You are faithful and just to forgive. We thank You that You spread our sins as far as the east is to the west and they will not be discussed again. We thank You that You are the "real deal" who does not offer counterfeit joy like the world does, but rather *eternal* joy. Thank You that You forgive us when we are disobedient. Give us grace to do the same with our own children. Help us to forgive ourselves for our past mistakes and to parent through freedom. Amen.

Week 6: Feeding the Green-Eyed Monster 2

Introduction

What is one way you "treat" yourself when you have a little extra money?

Discussion

☐ Ask members to describe a time they have overindulged their child with a video game, new clothes, candy, or similar item. What was the temporary motivation behind the purchase/gift?

☐ Discuss why it is important to acknowledge overindulgence.

cussing why they do it and the simple fact that they do it is crucial in stopping this weak parenting method.)

☐ Allow group members to discuss times when they have pur-
chased name-brand clothes, toys, or thrown elaborate parties that they could not afford and why they did so. Foster a discussion on what it means to be good stewards of what the Lord has afforded us, as well as avoiding the pressures that the world puts on us.

☐ Pass out index cards and have parents choose their favorite parenting scripture from Chapter 6 to write on the card. Their homework assignment will be to take extra care to adhere to the words in the verse but also to have a mini-devotion with their child about its importance. Have them post their cards on the fridge or bathroom mirror.

Prayer time
Allow the group members to break into smaller groups of two or three and pray for each others' children. Pray blessings over the children's futures, their health, their safety, and their choices.

Week 7: The Father Factor

Introduction
Ask participants to use one word to describe their earthly father. Then allow each to explain their response.

Discussion
☐ Ask members "Do your children have an active father-figure in their lives?" Regardless of their responses, ask them how it makes them feel. The goal is to foster a discussion of the hurt associated with the lack of a father figure in some single parents' lives, but also to acknowledge those fathers who have stepped

☐ Cite some of the statistics from Chapter 4 to the parents. Ask them which statistic surprised them the most.

☐ Ask members to share some words that would describe a "good" earthly father, in their opinion.

☐ Ask members if the words from question 3 accurately describe their Heavenly Father.

☐ Begin to move towards a discussion on what it is to have a Heavenly Father who loves us and our children. (The goal is to allow parents to see that even the lack of an earthly father does not doom their children to becoming a statistic. Our Heavenly Father's love is sufficient).

Prayer

Lord God, You know the hurt that many have experienced from their earthly fathers. You know the hurt that our children have seen. Father, allow us to release the anger we hold towards this absent father. Allow us to rest in knowing that You are sufficient. Help us not to worry about our son or daughter's future. Help us to know that You hold our children in the palm of Your hand and that they are safe there. Amen.

Week 8: The Father Factor 2

Introduction:

Review the previous week's discussion on fatherlessness, statistics, and memories of our own fathers. Did the Lord show any of the Moms anything this week in reference to last week's discussion?

Discussion

☐ What is the difference between the love of an earthly father (even a good one) and the love of our Heavenly Father? (Encourage the group to discuss how even the best of fathers are still human. They still have flaws and failures. Yet our Heavenly Father's love for us is perfect, never failing. He never disappoints or lets us down. He is dependable and consistent.)

☐ Begin a discussion on how to teach our children about our Heavenly Father. Daily prayer time, family devotions, conversations, and regular church attendance are just some of the ways to encourage our children to know more about the Lord. The God-sized hole in our children's lives can only be filled with God.

☐ Have every parent take the time to write a letter to their child,
either to be read by them immediately or when they are older. The letter should be one positive and encouraging, written to explain who they are in Christ Jesus, how much their Heavenly Father loves them, and how much their mother loves them.

☐ Have parents discuss practical ways to fill their child's love tank. Letter-writing, affirming words of love, scripture, surprise activities, and daily time spent together are just a few of the ways.

☐ Research Christian mentoring programs in your local community or through your church to help guide single parents who have no male role model in their children's lives.

Prayer Time
Have the parents focus their prayer time today on their children's futures. Have them pray for sensitivity to see when their children may be struggling with an absentee parent. Pray for wisdom about the right word to say to encourage their children. Also focus on praying for the absentee parent.

Week 9: Healthy Boundaries
Introduction
Begin by asking each parent to think of one other single parent in

parent to bring another single parent to your single moms ministry. Explain how important it is to reach out to those in our lives who may be hurting and not to assume that they will not come or are not interested.

Discussion

☐ Discuss the importance of emphasizing healthy boundaries in our homes. (Highlight our need to protect children physically, emotionally, and spiritually.)

☐ Discuss some of the pulls of today's world on our children.

☐ Have parents discuss some non-negotiables that have been set forth currently in their home. Encourage them to glean ideas from others in the group.

☐ As we begin to discuss positive parenting and healthy boundaries, it is important for parents to recognize their parenting style. Do any of the parents struggle with perfectionism? Controlling parent? Have the group discuss the dangers of this type of parenting.

☐ Each child will make mistakes. They will at some point disap-
point us. These mistakes do not always reflect our own poor parenting. Afford parents the opportunity to discuss their child's mistakes or discipline issues. Be sure to encourage the parents with the truth that all children make mistakes. Many parents need the opportunity to share in this area, as so many try to hide the failure, internalize, and become embarrassed or ashamed. Encourage the parents that this is a safe zone for them to share about the burdens they may be carrying.

Prayer Time

Father, we love You. We love Your word and its power in our lives.

children. We pray for guidance as we move forward with setting forth healthy boundaries in our homes. Help us to know what those non-negotiables in our home should be and give us strength to implement them. Make us wise and give us eyes to see those areas we may have been missing. Give us words to speak life and encouragement over our children. Help us guard our tongues that we would not discourage them or tear them down. Help us release the burden of perfectionism and place it all in your hands. Amen.

Week 10: Encouragement

Introduction
Begin by introducing all the new parents who were brought in from the last meeting's homework challenge. Next, allow each parent a moment to share what types of encouragement work for them when they are feeling a bit discouraged.

Discussion
☐ Have members discuss a time in their parenting journey when they have reached the end of their rope. What did it feel like?

☐ Discuss the feelings of loneliness that many single parents feel.

(As parents share, begin to encourage them that the Lord never leaves us or forsakes us.)

☐ Read Joshua 1:9 aloud. Discuss.

☐ Read Jeremiah 17:9 aloud. Foster a discussion on how our heart can deceive us. Focus on the feelings of loneliness, depression, discouragement, and anger that we can feel towards God or others and how these feelings are deceitful. Oftentimes we can allow our emotions to dictate our walk with the Lord, as well as our parenting techniques.

☐ Ask each single parent to write a letter of encouragement to a and to share some of those things that they would like to hear from others. Gather the letters and bring them to a local battered women's shelter, crisis pregnancy clinic, unwed mothers' home, or neighboring single parent ministry.

Prayer Time

During today's prayer time, break into pairs of two. Have each parent speak a word of encouragement over their prayer partner's life. Then focus on praying encouraging words over each other's lives.

Week 11: Encouragement

Introduction

Share with the group what you did with their letters of encouragement from last meeting and any special stories you may have heard as a result. Have the group share about how writing the letters made them feel.

Discussion

☐ Many parents hold themselves to such a high standard in parenting that they struggle to forgive themselves when they have made a parenting mistake. Have group discuss what this means to them.

☐ Read 2 Corinthians 5:17 aloud. This scripture gives us freedom that we are a new creation in Christ, that old things have been washed away. He makes all things new. Ask parents if there is something in their lives that they are struggling to forgive themselves for or struggling to believe was made new when they became Christians.

☐ The enemy is an expert at attempting to make us feel like failures as parents. What are some of the lies he has whispered in

You are a failure as a parent. You always mess things up. You will not have enough money. God will not provide. You are wasting your time praying.)

☐ Encourage participants to think of a time when God has provided in their lives against all odds. Allow them to share.

☐ Isaiah 43:19 proclaims that God is about to do something new, making pathways in the wilderness and rivers in the dry waste-land. As single parents, it is easy to get stuck in the desert, wandering around, feeling quite lost and alone. What is the one new thing that parents would like to see God do in their lives?

Prayer
Begin to pray for participants that the Lord would move according to His will and provide that new thing that they have been believing Him for. Pray for a refreshing and renewal over the each parent's life.

Week 12: The Four C's

Introduction
Begin by having each parent share one quirky or little-known fact about themselves. Be sure you join in the fun!

Discussion:
☐ It is said that early communication is the catalyst for great relationships between parent and child. Have the parents give an account of how they feel the lines of communication flow in their homes.

☐ Discuss ideas on what can be done differently. Focus on things that are working in other homes with similar aged children.

over lack of communication in their home and offer encouragement.

☐ Avoiding closed-end questions that can be answered with only a few words is an excellent way to get or keep conversation flowing. Have each group member think of one open-ended question that can be used in conversation with their child that would be age-appropriate for them.

☐ Why is it important for parents to remain consistent? Focus on comfort and safety of our children. Also be sure to point out that our Heavenly Father is always consistent as He parents us, using His word as a constant guide for our lives.

☐ Allow parents to discuss "moody" parenting. Have they struggled in this area with the weight of financial and parenting pressures?

Prayer

Pray that members may remove anything from their lives that hinders them in communication with their children, whether it be anger, insecurity, exhaustion, or others. Pray for the Holy Spirit's guidance with communication to our children and a constant prompting for us to initiate conversations.

Week 13: The Four C's

Introduction

Begin by reviewing last week's lesson on communication and consistency. Have group members share any breakthroughs they have experienced since the last meeting.

Discussion

'☐ Clarity is imperative in parenting as our children grow and mature. Have parents give an example of a rule in their home that they have had to adjust as their child aged (or that they will have to adjust in the future).

☐ Parents can sometimes view a pre-teen's desire for explanation as disobedience when it really is simply a sign of age progression and independence. Have parents in the group struggled with this?

☐ Our parenting, our lives, our future success is dependent upon our walk with the Lord and daily time with Him. Have parents discuss their daily Bible time. (Be sure to be sensitive to those parents who are struggling in this area, encouraging new ideas on getting the time in. Also stress that time with the Lord is not mean to be a rigid, legalistic routine, but rather an exciting and energizing time to pray about concerns, hopes, etc.)

☐ The Bible says to "pray without ceasing." Have parents discuss what that means. Have them focus on not only their parenting, but their lives in general. (The key is that parents understand that we can pray all day, anywhere, and it is simply "talking to God." We can do so in our cars on lunch break, at the red light, or waiting in line to pick up our children from school.) Our prayer time is about a reverence and relationship with the Lord.

Prayer

In today's prayer time allow parents to just sit in silence for a bit. Allow them time to just get alone before the Lord. This may have been their only opportunity for the day to just be quiet and still before Him. After you have allowed time close in a prayer that each member would draw closer to the Lord, that relationships with the Lord would be strengthened. Feel free to allow another parent to lead in the prayer.

Week 14: Bible Basics

Introduction

Announce that as a group you would like to do an activity where you can all serve the community. Discuss ideas and set an upcoming date. (Ideas can include: free car wash at a local grocery store or fast-food restaurant, visiting a nursing home to read to the elderly, bringing snacks to local police and fire departments, writing letters of encouragement to teachers, and countless others!)

Discussion

☐ We can all struggle with being self-absorbed. What are some ways we can teach our children to focus on others? Why is it important?

☐ The Golden Rule encourages us to treat others kindly. Have members discuss how this coincides with teaching our children manners.

☐ What are some manners that participants are teaching their children?

☐ Have members discuss the value of hard work by sharing a time in their childhood when they first learned of its significance.

☐ Have members discuss some ways they are teaching their children about hard work.

☐ Close by discussing the difference between working "as unto the Lord" and "perfectionism." Be sure to focus on perfectionism as a bondage—a standard for which could never measure up. Rather working "as unto the Lord" is giving Him our very best.

Prayer

Father, we thank You for all You have revealed in our lives through this study. We thank You that You love our children far more than we ever could. We thank You that You are a consistent "daddy" to us and our children. We love You. We pray for continued wisdom. Remind us gently to pray daily. Help us to pray over our children. Help us to pray about our children. Help us to teach our children to pray. Draw us close to You. We love You, Lord. Amen.

Now spend some time praying over each family, specifically for the parent and their children.

ABOUT THE AUTHOR

Jennifer Barnes Maggio

At 17 years old, Jennifer Maggio found herself a homeless, unwed, teen mom who had little hope or future. Over the next seven years, she discovered the hardships of single parenting—finances, parenting woes, and emotional stability. Though her story takes many twists and turns, she ultimately found the hope and freedom that only a relationship with Jesus Christ can bring. She went on to become an 11-time Circle of Excellence winner in Corporate America providing financial counseling to families and quickly scaled the corporate ladder to become a successful executive in a Fortune 500 company. Several years ago, she left the corporate world behind to pursue her God-given passion for ministering to single moms.

Maggio not only runs one of the largest single moms ministries in the country through the generosity of her local church, Healing Place Church in Baton Rouge, Louisiana, but she is also the founder of The Life of a Single Mom Ministries. TLSM Ministries is the nation's fastest-growing nonprofit, founded to educate and equip churches on how to best meet the needs of single parents in their communities through support groups, events, and resources.

An award-winning author and dynamic speaker who leaves audiences everywhere riveted and inspired, Maggio is the author of the critically-acclaimed *Overwhelmed: The Life of a Single Mom* and founder of *Overwhelmed: The Single Moms Magazine*. Her second book, *The Church and the Single Mom*, has taken the church world by storm as she challenges every Christian to get involved in the lives of single parents in their communities.

Maggio is currently a columnist with *Single Parents Town, Halo Magazine, BizyMoms*, and *Crosswalk* and has written dozens of articles for publications worldwide. She is a regular on radio and television and has appeared on The 700 Club, Daystar Television, Focus on the Family, Moody Radio, Alive in Christ, Power Women, and countless others.

For more information or to book an appearance, visit http://www.thelifeofasinglemom.com.